THE
ROCKING CHAIR TEST

A STEP TO STEP GUIDE TO BECOMING #FUTUREYOU

ANDY FELL

Book Design by: Aeyshaa

Illustrations by: Jessamy Gee

CONTENTS

INTRODUCTION

Seminyak, Bali, Indonesia – September 29th, 2016

Everything changed when my 50th birthday came around. Well, not immediately, but the decisions I made that day initiated a process that eventually led to fundamental change in my life.

I had been working in financial services since graduating from university and often dreamt of being my own boss, running my own business, and most importantly, having time/financial freedom. Up until that point, I hadn't done much to make that dream come true. I had taken redundancy from a major bank in the United Kingdom at the height of the global financial crisis and took a few tentative steps toward starting my own business called *Expect2Win*. However, soon thereafter, another bank in Australia recruited me, and so, I returned to the world of banking I was so familiar with—except this time, it was on the opposite side of the world.

My dream was exactly that: a dream. And if I had continued on the same path, it was in danger of staying that way for the rest of my working life.

And so, on my 50th birthday, my eldest daughter, Emma, did one of the most amazing things anyone has ever done for me. One morning, while we celebrated in a private villa with close friends, my wife, Leona, and I took an early morning walk on the beach. Whilst we walked, Emma thoughtfully hung 50 photos from 50 different moments of my life in the villa's living area. Between each photo was a small card with a handwritten speech pinned to the strings that stretched across the room. Every person that celebrated with us that day wrote more than one of these cards. Some were deep and meaningful, while others were fun and silly. Each one began in the same manner: "I love Andy because..."

When Leona and I got back from the beach walk, I was shocked at the beautiful sight my eyes were met with as soon as I entered the villa. I walked around, reading each card and studying the photos of wonderful memories I had made over the past 50 years with tears in my eyes. It was both a heartfelt and creative gesture. While I toured the room, I was subconsciously engaged in the *Sir Richard Branson Rocking Chair Test* in which you imagine yourself as a 90-year-old in a rocking chair, reflecting on the life you've lived. It was at that point that I began to question what I had achieved so far in my life and what I could achieve during all the years to come. I knew I had a long way to go to be satisfied with my accomplishments and to even near the limits of my own potential.

50 photos and 50 comments fundamentally changed my life. These were the sparks that ignited a burning desire within me to achieve more, do more, and ultimately *be* more.

What did I WANT to be saying to MYSELF?

Sir Richard Branson asks you to think about what you would say to your 90-year-old self in that rocking chair. And so, I thought and pondered upon this concept. Did I want to be saying: "If only I had done this" or "I wish I had done that"? Did I want to say, "I could have done this" or "I should have done that"? Surely, the answer was *no*.

I decided to achieve more in the next 25 years of my life than I had in the previous 50 years. To do that, I needed to clearly define my purpose and break free of my own self-limiting beliefs to make room for significant change.

Many would consider my career to have been a success, but personally, I felt as though I still had so much more to achieve and give. I wanted to take my knowledge, winning habits, routines, frameworks, and leadership techniques out into the world. I encountered far too many people who were trapped in a job they didn't enjoy and working for a boss who didn't value or respect them. Yet, these people didn't have the required, positive self-beliefs or confidence to create change in their lives. They lacked the courage to follow their dreams. They bought into their own self-limiting perceptions and were convinced that their current circumstances paid the bills, which was worth the sacrifices they had made.

To help others believe in themselves and stretch further than their comfort zones allow, I had to go first and model what I was preaching. When I talked about my thinking, many people advised me to play it safe, stick with what I knew and hang on to what I had. I was urged to think of the risks and consequences associated with my decision. In the hope of persuading me, many people shared the failure rate of start-ups, and focused on what I could lose as opposed to what I could gain.

Those closest to me gave me the greatest level of support and encouragement and were the wind beneath my wings. Leona gave me the confidence to reach for what I dreamed of, and for that, I am forever grateful.

So, it was decided. I had made a commitment and it was time to 'go'.

After returning to Australia from Bali, I began to journal with a focus on two specific aspects of my life. First, I wrote about my purpose and the vision I had for the remainder of my life. From this, clarity emerged.

I realized that my purpose is as follows: *To help as many people as possible strive to reach their true potential by being the wind beneath their wings so they can soar to new heights.*

Second, I focused on the more practical side of thinking by creating a plan for my own business, identifying the problems I wanted to help people overcome and what I needed to establish to hit the ground running. How would I serve my audience? How did I intend to make a difference?

6 months later, I left the corporate world and founded GiFT631.

I grew up in a house that was numbered 631 and I wanted my parents and grandfather's legacy to live on in my business. During my journaling process, I had wrestled with a few business names until GiFT fell into place. It was an acronym for the following words:

Growth - Personal, team and business. Without growth, we stagnate and decline.

Inspiration - Inspiring others to reach their true potential by guiding them from where they are to where they want to be. I call this place 'FutureYou.'

Fulfilment - Helping people pass the *rocking chair test* by finding their own value and living true to their passions and purpose.

Transformation - Helping people, teams, and businesses pivot, evolve, and soar.

Once I took the plunge, I went from being the general manager of a big bank to a self-employed founder of a start-up. Early on in this transition, I immediately recognized the value of the habits, routines, and frameworks I had developed over the past 30 years. As a new entrepreneur involved in the world of self-improvement, I have continued to develop, recreate, and implement these habits, routines, and frameworks for increased and long-term success, and now consider them to be my *success system*. In essence, this system helps me set and work through big goals, develop and sustain a 'champion's mindset', take consistent, high-value action, and seek ongoing improvement to ensure I am always moving forward and improving. The more I modify these routines, the more robust they become, thus giving me the confidence to stretch my thinking and aim for bigger goals.

Now, I have the pleasure and privilege of sharing these habits, routines, and frameworks through my work as a coach, consultant, speaker, facilitator, and writer. I constantly witness the difference they can make, but only for those who are willing to consistently apply them and do the work.

Nothing changes without action.

SECTION 1
THE FOUNDATION GIFTS

The purpose of this book is to share knowledge in the most simple, practical, and actionable way. I see each framework, habit, routine or idea that I share as a GiFT from me to you.

The initial ones in this section are the foundation stones to enable you to get maximum benefit from the ones that follow. They provide some of the basic thinking and practices that set me up for success. By embedding them and absorbing the concepts you can set a platform for everything that follows.

I advise you to read the book with a pen and highlighter in hand. Have a journal or notebook of your own by your side. Mark things that resonate with you and write as many notes in the margins as you deem necessary.

Read the book GiFT by GiFT. Stop after each one, reflect, and think about the ways in which you can apply the knowledge to your own life. To have value, apply the knowledge. To help you with this, consider and then answer the questions. Tackle all the activities. Be #allin as these GiFTs when applied consistently can make a big difference.

Some of the habits, routines, and frameworks will fall into place quickly, while others will need persistence to work until they become second nature.

As you read along, I want to encourage you to adapt any of the teachings as needed. What works brilliantly for me, may not work in the same way for you. See the advice I provide here as *thought starters*—a guide to help you get going, restart, accelerate, or transform your journey. What matters most is that you create and design your own success system that's built on the habits and routines that serve you.

The only way to start is to start. Let's work through the foundation GiFTs in section one.

1) The GiFT from Mozart

As the manager of a big and busy branch of a major UK bank, I was caught in a whirlwind that controlled me. Time to think was scarce and it always seemed like my thoughts were disorderly and chaotic. And so, my response was to run from it all—ever faster with no real finish line ahead. I would arrive home every evening tired and questioning what—if anything—I had achieved during the day.

As part of my personal development, I attended a conference and heard a story which resonated with me and over time, altered the course of my life. The story taught me an important lesson that later prompted me to create a habit. This habit became central to my success, enabled me to regain control in the short-term, and allowed me to find breakthroughs and success in the long-term.

The story I heard was about the famous composer, Mozart. Apparently, Mozart suffered from *composer's cramp*. To overcome it, he walked alone through the beautiful countryside listening to birds, watching deer, squirrels, and other animals, all while inhaling the calming scents of the forest. Isolated from the world and free from distraction, he was able to compose music in his head once more.

After reflecting on the story and its meaning, I scheduled an appointment in my calendar to reflect on my life the way Mozart did to release himself from the mental block he was experiencing. Of course, the appointment was purely for myself, by myself, and with myself.

Essentially, it became my daily time to think, away from distractions and the pressure of the moment. It became my first winning habit. I call it Mozart time and its scheduled daily.

I used that time to reflect on a vast array of subjects, ranging from controlling the whirlwind that was my life at the time to setting goals, to thoughts on how to become a better leader, how to build a better team, environment, and culture to how to coach my team and improve our approach to the things that matter most. In essence, this quiet time allows me to think and ask myself questions to find a way forward in all aspects of my life.

I avoid distractions or the possibility of interruptions. I am away from my laptop and my phone. If my phone is with me, it is on silent. Although I love music, this is one time when I value silence as it an opportunity to slow down in a fast-paced world and escape the daily whirlwind.

This habit has sparked the thoughts that developed into many—if not most—of the *GiFTs* contained within this book. My purpose and business name emerged from this habit. Business ideas, strategies, leadership, and coaching practices emerged from this habit. It enables me to reflect and build on ideas, thoughts, and all the things I learn from others.

I have come to the realisation that greatness requires stillness. From stillness comes clarity, and from clarity comes insight, innovation, breakthrough, and success.

A daily dose of *Mozart time* is my time to create this stillness. Everything else flows from it.

Questions for you:

What does your average day look like?

Are you caught in a whirlwind of your own, when time flies by and you question how much you have achieved?

When do you give yourself permission to stop and think?

When you do, how do you capture your thoughts and ideas?

Actions for you:

Get your diary and mark out 15/20 minutes a day. Your time.

Give this time a name (your version of Mozart time).

Have your journal with you, your phone on silent and your laptop turned off.

Explain to the people around you what you are doing and why so you avoid interruptions.

Mozart-time questions for you:

If you need help to get started, here are a few broad questions you can consider.

1. What do I want to achieve over the next 6/12/18 months?

2. What would my ideal job/life look like in 5 years' time?

3. How do I become a better............(leader/salesperson/ sportsperson/coach/parent/add your own categories)

4. What am I great at?

5. What would I love to work on over the next 6/12/18 months to be a better version of me?

6. What do I love doing and how can I do more of it? How can I turn it into a job, business or side hustle?

7. How do I build a better team?

8. How do I serve my customers better?

9. How do I spend less time at work? How do I become more efficient in all I do?

10. What should I do differently today?

11. When am I at my happiest and why?

12. How do I pass the Sir Richard Branson test? What do I want to be saying to myself when I am sitting in my rocking chair?

2) The GiFT of journaling

Journaling goes hand in hand with *Mozart time* but needs a space of its own. Your journal is the ideal place to answer the questions posed as part of the previous GiFT. It is a great place to start writing down your own questions too.

Journaling is not limited to my formalised *Mozart time*, as my journal is always with me, and thoughts and ideas can pop up at any time. My mind moves quickly and sometimes I was losing thoughts before I had captured them.

I am predominantly action-orientated, an activist who wants to get things done. Therefore, my journal is a crucial tool to note thoughts and ideas that are not yet mature enough to become part of a plan or strategy.

I also separate my journal from the notebooks I take to meetings, conferences, and events because I do not want my thoughts, feelings, and ideas to get lost in day-to-day business.

Eventually, I published my own *#whatwinnersdo* journal, which has become central to my success. In the journal, I wrote an introductory page which captures the essence of the power of journaling and the impact it can have when practiced consistently over time. Here it is:

"Throughout my life I have met so many people for whom dreams have stayed as dreams and good intentions have never turned into goals and actions. By contrast people who move in the direction of the life they want, create winning habits and routines. Journaling is one such routine.

I truly believe that 'greatness requires stillness' and at regular intervals you need to slow down to speed up. It is easy to get caught up in the day-to-day frenzy and not stop to consider what we want from our lives. We are here for a short time. Let's work out how to get the most from the time we have available.

To do that, I am a passionate believer in Mozart time - time for ourselves without technology or interruption. Sitting with a journal and a mind free of clutter is where stillness turns into clarity. In turn clarity turns to creativity and breakthrough.

Journaling has a daily element, for example in the morning I capture what I am happy and grateful for and in the evening, I note the best thing that has happened each day. At other times I am future focused, thinking about my desired future state and how I live the life of my dreams. My business, GiFT631, was born out of journaling. Journaling helped me establish the purpose, the key pillars, the name and coaching frameworks. The practical and actionable strategies and stories I use in my speaking, writing, coaching and mentoring have also developed through this quiet, reflective time.

This journal can be the wind beneath your wings to enable you to soar to new heights. Use it daily. The only way to start is to start."

In essence, the GiFTs within this book started as a thought usually prompted by somebody or something else. *Mozart time* gave me space to think about how it could add value to my life and having a journal meant I could capture and build on the thought. The ongoing art of journaling turned thoughts into ideas, strategies, frameworks and actions that I now share with you.

3) The GiFT of L/C+10%!

A one-time colleague, Dave Koziupa, once shared with me another story:

"The top 100 people in an industry gather for a conference. The No1 person is asked to go on stage and share all the secrets of her success. She does it. She shares all her winning practices and habits. After her presentation, she is asked why she isn't concerned about giving all her secrets away. The No1 replies that, in her view, at least 50% of the audience weren't listening and out of the rest, only a small number will have the strength and discipline needed to change their behaviour in any way. She ends by saying she will still be No1 the following year. She was—and by an even greater margin, for that matter."

Initially, when I heard this story, I was disappointed in human behaviour. How can someone so successful openly share exactly what she is doing with the full knowledge that most others in her industry will do nothing differently? To me, it made no sense at all. Why are people's eyes, ears, and minds so closed off to new learning, particularly when it is shared by someone who is currently more successful than they are?

I then saw the opportunity. What if I become one of the few people who do something new by applying the knowledge that has been shared with them?

I decided to seek successful people at every level— entrepreneurs, individuals I admired, leaders, companies, writers, and teams. I wanted to learn about and absorb all the things that made them successful. I looked at different sectors and parts of the world and saw constant learning as a competitive advantage—as long as the learning was implemented.

I captured all my insights in my journal. During my daily *Mozart time,* I had the opportunity to think about what I had seen, heard, and read, and then add my own ideas to it all.

By taking this approach and applying the learning to my current and future plans, not only did my performance improve, but my team's performance did as well. This is common sense, but certainly not common practice., Too many people are closed off to new ideas while others let their ego get in the way. I was taught that ego is the enemy of achievement.

Others have a cynical view of success, putting it down to factors like luck, or creating self-limiting beliefs about why they cannot be successful, why it is easier for others or that they have tried it before and it's not for them. I believe this is why so few people actually changed as a result of listening to the No1. I am sure phrases like 'It's easier for her.' 'I've tried it before' or 'that wouldn't work for me as my customers are different' would have been heard at the coffee break following the session!

My mantra is to *learn, copy, and add my own 10% winning edge* (L/C+10%). Learn from people who are achieving success in what they do, copy what they are doing, and then add 10% to improve upon the practice. This mentality and approach are simply about seeking continuous improvement.

Why invest time, effort and/or money to reinvent the wheel, when others are already operating at a high standard and achieving great success?

Together, *Mozart time*, journaling and L/C+10% are a great combination and helped significantly over many years. Then, at a client offsite, one of the attendees, Paul Tucker, advanced my thinking further. Paul suggested that sometimes, you can copy a winning behaviour, while at other times, you need to *adapt the practice to find your own 10%* (L/A+10%). He was implying that in some situations you can find great learnings from others, but a direct copy may not be appropriate. The idea or practice has value, but you need to take some Mozart time to work through how to apply it in your current circumstance and/or environment.

Feedback is the breakfast of champions and I love to see others helping me improve my own thinking and content. As you work through this book, please feel free to do the same. As you work with the GiFTs, adapt them as needed to make them work for you and those around you.

The critical factor is having a relentless appetite to learn and improve by seeking out successful people, practices and systems and then acting in your own environment, so you continue to move forward and improve. Do this in as many ways as possible from formal learning to reading, to audio books, podcasts, YouTube videos, articles, LinkedIn and other social content to e-zines, blogs, courses, seminars and having a coffee or breakfast with someone you admire and respect.

Questions for you:

Do you actively seek new learning? How?

How and where do you capture the learnings?

How do you reflect and review those learnings?

What do you do with the new knowledge?

Think back to a recent book you read, video you watched, podcast you listened to, coffee you had with some you admire, course or seminar you attended. What did you learn? What have you done differently because of the learning?

4) The GiFT from Plato's cave (L/C+10% in action)

It's one thing to listen to people share their valuable insights, ideas, strategies, and practices, but it is another to adopt them, put them into practice, and work toward integrating them into your winning routines and habits.

For a long time, I thought about the 100 people gathered at that conference. I was sure that more than a few of the audience would try at least one thing that the speaker shared. Even if that was the case, why didn't the new learning stick? Why do only a select few change their behaviour to create new habits? Why do the rest disregard important information given to them by successful people or why do they give up on what they have heard and revert to their previous behaviours?

This is my theory.

Imagine living your whole life in a cave of total darkness. One day, someone lets you out and you see that it's a beautiful, sunny day. What happens to your eyes?

You are temporarily blinded. It feels uncomfortable and it takes time for your vison to adjust to the light you've been unfamiliar with. You'll feel an undeniable urge to run back into the comfort of the cave. It is an environment you know and one that feels safe. There is no growth and no progress but at least it's familiar and at least you are in control.

However, what happens when you resist this temptation? You hold your position in the sun and tolerate the initial discomfort. Your eyes adjust. After a few moments, you see a stunning vista ahead of you and no longer feel a desire to return to the dark, cold, and dingy cave. You want to move forward and explore. You see a better life ahead and want to move toward it, even though it's unfamiliar and new. You push through regardless.

Personal growth and development are the same. First, we need to move out of our comfort zone (the cave) and embrace the uncanny. Change is uncomfortable, so it's normal to try to explain why this new behaviour doesn't work, and immediately revert back to our old, average habits. However, when we keep working, testing, adapting, and persisting, our 'eyes adjust', and we establish a new and improved habit.

Be willing to make mistakes as you test and learn. Very early in my business career my then boss, Tony Schofield, the company's Managing Director, said to me, "The only people who don't make mistakes are the people who don't do anything." He encouraged me to live an action orientated life, be willing to give things a go and learn from them. He also said that when the time came for me to lead others, it was important I created an environment that encouraged others to do the same. The path to success involves mistakes.

When we are forced out from the cave, whether it be through the loss of a job or a failure of a business, we have no choice than to be comfortable with being uncomfortable. At these points, creating and improving winning habits are essential for progress and growth, or else the temporary blindness turns into anxiety, overwhelm, and a negative spiral that inhibits us from moving forward and reaching our ultimate potential.

But why do so many people wait until they are forced from the cave before they seek new and improved behaviours, habits, and routines? Surely, it is best to be in control and search for continuous improvement from a position of strength. Otherwise, complacency can become an unwanted companion. I see complacency as the first step to failure.

5) The success formula GiFT

Success is built on repeated, simple practices and frameworks. Doing something once adds limited value, doing it consistency builds expertise and ultimately mastery. Discipline is therefore critical to ensure new approaches do not fizzle out and we return to our cave.

Success means different things to different people. My unique definition of success is centred on my purpose, desired legacy and what I want to achieve to lead a happy and fulfilled life. It is some-thing I think about frequently as part of my Mozart time. When I make decisions, I ask myself whether the outcome will take me in the direction I want to take my life and make a positive difference to those I care about.

However, I meet lots of people who are lost in the day to day. They do not know or have not given themselves the time or space to really think about what success could look like for them. They have a feeling they want more but do not know exactly what it is or how to go after it.

After my 50th birthday, I needed more clarity on firstly what success looked like. I want to pass the rocking chair test. Secondly, I wanted a structure to help me get there. Finally, I wanted a formula that provided a structure for others to help them move in the direction they wanted. Something that would give them the confidence to back themselves and go for it. Over time, the GiFT631 success formula evolved as follows:

Success = Goals + Mindset + Action x Debrief

S=G+M+(AxD).

Goals: Goals give a sense of direction and a purpose. They motivate us, particularly goals that are big and clear. Great goals stretch our thinking, require us to be entirely committed, dedicated, action-orientated, innovative, and resourceful. Goals that take us some distance out of our 'cave' and require us to feel that initial discomfort.

Mindset: Our mindset, attitude, and belief system make a big difference to our success or otherwise. We need to be positive, optimistic, resilient, and persistent. When we feel this way, we have the confidence to take bold action and keep going when things are tough and we are faced with setbacks and disappointments. When we don't feel great, it is easy to stay where we are and accept 'our lot' in life.

I believe our mindset can be represented by our self-talk. We all talk to ourselves and each day our success is either aided or abetted by the quality of this self-talk. There is an inner conversation going on between our inner champion and our inner critic. One says, *"I can do this"* and that *"anything is possible",* whereas the other chips away at our confidence, convincing us that we are, amongst many other things, *"not good or smart enough."*

In challenging times when our confidence is low, this inner critic can dominate our self-talk which can lead to self-doubt. We can overthink and procrastinate. In these moments, the cave appears the safest and best place to be, but it also means opportunities are unseen, missed, and lost. We get frustrated and this further reinforces our negative self-talk and creates an unwanted spiral.

When our mindset is strong, the reverse happens. Our inner champion fuels our belief that we can achieve our goals and what we want. We need to feed our inner champion daily to ensure it stays strong, positive and dominant.

Action: There are two types of actions that are critical to our success, both of which are high value and need to be prioritised.

The first series of actions are those that work on our mindset. They help us get into an ideal performance state where our confidence and belief system are working for us.

The second type are the high value actions or activities that move us toward our goals. These have high impact, purpose, and meaning. Many people talk about the 80/20 rule and then get completely absorbed in the 80% of actions that are reactive, low in value, and lack meaningful connection to their goals. This is the whirlwind I described being caught in before implementing *Mozart time.* I was busy and was taking action, but I lacked control and prioritisation. I was reactive and responding to what others needed as opposed to being focused on what mattered most. You may be reacting to your latest email, text, or social media message, allowing it to drive you, or you may be caught in a whirlwind of endless meetings and over-committing to things that add little value to your overall goals in life.

As Goethe said, "The things that matter most must never be at the mercy of the things that matter least."

Debrief: The initial success formula stopped there. It was simply S=G+M+A. I then realised adding the debrief was the +10% winning edge. Yehuda Shinar, author of *Winning,* once told me that "winners debrief more than the average." Once we have undertaken a meaningful action set aside a few minutes to pause and reflect on what happened. Ask yourself a few key questions about the action. It is as important to analyse the root cause of success as it is to find the root cause of disappointment. If the action has gone well, why was that? How can you learn from it and do more of it? Equally debriefing an action that hasn't gone as we wanted allows us to identify areas for development and further improvement.

By consistently debriefing, we constantly enhance what we do and accelerate in the direction of our goals.

SECTION 1-SUMMARY

These are the foundation GiFTs to help you create a solid platform to move your life forward.

Quality and consistent *Mozart time* also enables you to think about the life you want and the goals you need to create a clear sense of direction. It is about creating space to think, journal and ask yourself questions.

"Life begins at the edge of our comfort zone" is a favourite mantra. Moving forward requires us to operate outside of our 'cave'. One way to make that easier is to learn from others who are already achieving great success generally or display certain characteristics or practices that you want to understand and develop.

"Success leaves clues" is another favourite mantra. Most of the answers we seek are already out there. We just need to look and take advantage of the success and learnings of others. Every interaction we have also provides an opportunity to learn and grow.

However, knowledge without action is useless. We need to apply the learning. As Arnold Schwarzenegger once said, "No one got muscles watching me work-out."

By doing this repeatedly, L/C+10% developed and its application has been a great accelerator in my life.

To create change and get started on a new or improved path, follow the GiFT631 success formula: S = G+M+(AxD)

Success is dependent on each element of the success formula working together. For example, what held me back were the times my inner critic was overpowering my inner champion. This self-doubt and lack of confidence made me more timid with regards to goal setting and the actions I was prepared to take. Confidence is a fragile bird that can easily be knocked out of flight. The mindset *GiFTs* in section 3 build my confidence and power up my inner champion, so I believe I can achieve my goals. When my confidence is high, my belief system is strong, and I am ready to set and take on increasingly bigger goals. I am also willing to take more decisive action.

The rest of the book works through the different elements of the success formula, providing a series of simple, practical and actionable GiFTs for you to utilise. We start with goals.

There are many great goal setting and goal-achieving techniques and practices. I have distilled them into the ones that work best for me and my clients.

GOALS!

6) The GiFT of vision and vision boards:

Before we get into the more practical side of goal setting, let's allow ourselves the opportunity to do some blue sky thinking. This is free thinking without applying any constraints like time, money, age or current circumstances.

Take your time to work through this exercise.

With a journal in hand and no possibility of distraction or interruption, think about the life you want to live. Then answer the following questions:

What would you be doing if time and money were no object?

Where would you be living?

Who would you be with?

What is your dream job, business or career?

How would you spend your leisure time?

Where would you travel?

Would you live by the ocean, in the mountains, or in a slick city apartment?

Would you head toward the sun or the snow?

What difference would you make in the world?

Who would you help, why, and how?

What is your dream life?

Add any other questions that are important to you to the list, and answer those as well. You may want to look back at some of the questions we posed to kick-start your Mozart time.

Your responses can be as aspirational as you want. By returning to these questions frequently, you may add and change some of your initial responses. Some answers may excite you more than others. That is an indication of what matters most right now and what is worth striving for.

Start there.

Can you see yourself living this life in your mind? If you want to live for 3 months every year in Portugal's beautiful Algarve, can you see yourself sitting on the beach, swimming in the sea, or enjoying lunch with a glass of wine in a marina cafe? Can you sense the warm sun on your skin? Who are you with? What are they saying? What are they doing? How does it feel?

Some people love this type of visualisation and find that it comes naturally. For others, their minds wander, and they struggle to see such an image clearly and repeatedly for it to inspire any action. If you are this type of person, I recommend creating a vision board that includes a series of visual reminders of your desired future state. Place this vision board in a high-traffic area in your home so that it serves as a constant reminder of what you want your future to look like. Make it fun, aspirational, colourful, and eye-catching. It needs to be something you are proud to talk about with your friends and family.

Your vision board is essentially your bucket-list of things you want to achieve and do in life, with the exception that some may have more permanence. It can include pictures of your ideal home, kitchen, or bathroom, the places you want to go on holiday, you crossing the finish line of a marathon, or attending the winter Olympics.

By way of an example, I have pictures of everything I want to achieve in life, including a stunning apartment overlooking the ocean, wild rhinos, famous cricket grounds, the Canadian Rockies, Japan, and the front of a bookstore in which this very book sits comfortably in the window.

Perceive visualisation and vision boards as complementary to each other. The more of this type of imagery—physical, on our devices, or in our minds—the better.

Actions for you:

Put the book down and schedule some *Mozart time* with your journal in hand.

Take your time and work through the questions listed above. Be aspirational.

Revisit the questions at least once.

From the questions, start to think about images that represent the answers.

Start to collect pictures – these could be postcards, images cut from travel, style, home or other magazines, ones that you download or from any other sources that work for you.

Put them together as a vision-board. Keep adding to it as you think of new things.

Place this vision board somewhere in your home and/or office where you see it regularly.

If you choose a virtual vision board, make sure you are prompted to look at it daily.

When ready, talk about this vision board with key people in your life. Pick people who believe in you, support you and want to see you grow and succeed! People who lift you up.

7) The GiFT of SMUUT goals – the power of going big!

When you look at your vision board and answer the last question in the previous GiFT, look to create a short paragraph that describes what a great life looks like. I refer to this as a 'desired future state.' I call it #futureyou. It is something aspirational, something to aim for that stretches beyond the ordinary.

Thinking and journaling about our desired future state is one way to put the bigger picture into perspective, but how do we start on the journey toward it?

Many training courses encourage you to set SMART goals (specific, measurable, achievable, realistic, and timebound). However, I struggle with this concept.

I am in favour of S *(specific)*, M *(measurable)*, and T *(timebound)*.

Being *specific* means having clarity. Clarity matters because it gives us a sense of where we want to go. It allows us to develop a laser like focus to ensure we stretch for our goals. *Measurable* simply means implementing a method to measure progress towards the goal and ultimately whether it has been achieved. It allows you to identify where you are making progress, which provides the opportunity to celebrate appropriate milestones and make changes to your actions as necessary. Finally, *timebound* helps mobilize goals. I once read that "a goal without a deadline is a wish", which perfectly captures the need to add a date to a goal.

Over time, I found myself questioning the A *(achievable)* and the R *(realistic)*. Why set achievable and realistic goals? Does a SMART goal mentality significantly move our lives forward? Does it create and unlock creativity and innovation? Does a SMART goal demand focus and attention because of its size and the effort needed to achieve it? If everyone sets SMART goals, will it lead to mediocrity?

Often, SMART goals are based on past achievements with a little bit added. Rather than basing a goal on what has happened in the past, why not think about the opportunity that lies ahead?

Michael Angelo once said, "The greater danger for most of us lies not in setting our aim too high and falling short; but in setting our aim too low, and achieving our mark."

Even if the SMART goal is achieved, it does not take us that far out of the cave.

I decided to set my aim high accepting I might fall short, as opposed to setting and achieving SMART but limiting goals.

For a number of years, I spoke about UNSMART goals—big goals that are unrealistic and seem unachievable. UNSMART goals help us access a more innovative and resourceful part of ourselves. We must think big, seek creative solutions, and commit more focused effort.

The purpose is less about whether we achieve the goal, and more about how we re-program our thinking. It is about a growth mindset. Those who commit to big goals get further than those who set small goals, as long as consistent and focused action is taken.

Let's operationalize this concept using numbers to illustrate the point.

Person A sets a goal of 40 and achieves 75% of it = 30.

Person B sets a SMART goal of 10 and achieves 120% of it = 12.

Who would you rather be? Has person A failed because they 'only' achieved 75% of a big goal? They have certainly gone a lot further than person B.

Two things have happened for me since I formed *GiFT631*.

1) While working with the leadership team at Exeter Insurance in the Southwest of England, I talked about UNSMART goals. The team liked the approach but not the name I had for it. And so, they renamed it SMUUT goals, which stood for *specific, measurable, unachievable, unrealistic,* and *timebound.* From that moment forward, I use the term SMUUT goals to describe big, stretching goals that seem well out of my current reach.

2) Busy people may find the SMUUT approach to goals overwhelming. And so, a process was needed to help people keep going, particularly when they reached what Professor Damian Hughes describes as the *messy middle*. This is the stage when the initial energy and motivation has dimmed, but a distance to reach the finish line still remains. I needed to find a way of breaking down SMUUT goals to ensure people avoided overwhelm. I knew I needed to evidence how you can make a big goal appear possible by breaking it down into more manageable pieces. One day I was thinking about 631 and for some reason reversed the numbers in my journal. When I looked at the numbers 1+3+6 it gave me the answer. The way to make big goals appear small.

8) The GiFT of 1+3+6 – the power of breaking down your goals, part 1

The sheer magnitude of a SMUUT goal can create a sense of overwhelm that translates into a lack of belief. When this happens, big dreams stay exactly as that: dreams. Instead of starting on the journey to achievement, we condition our minds to believe that it is too big and there is too much to do so we do nothing. Another challenge is the logical/analytical side of our brain wants to know the *how*, as in how can we achieve that goal? At the start, we cannot answer that question, or else it wouldn't fit the definition of a SMUUT goal in the first place. If we allow the logical/analytical side of the brain to take-over, we will start to reduce the size/scale of the goal until it represents a SMART not a SMUUT goal. One that is small enough we know exactly how to do it.

We also need a process to prevent energy/enthusiasm from fizzling out when immediate results are not seen.

In my *#whatwinnersdo* journal, 631 became 136, which then became 1+3+6:

The 1 - Establish one purpose/SMUUT goal. Clarify what matters most and what you want to achieve. This can be a desired future state or a big life goal, such as running your first marathon, starting a local business, purchasing your dream home, moving to Hawaii, paying off your mortgage by a certain age or date, or leaving your job to become an entrepreneur. Represent the 1 on your vision board and in as many other places as you can. See it frequently.

The 3 - Break this big SMUUT goal down into 3 sub-goals. By doing this you create some milestones which are important. They provide a sense of accomplishment and reasons to celebrate. This is important as success breeds success, and we like to feel we are making progress. It can help create a sense of momentum, so we keep moving forward at pace. Once you achieve a sub-goal, replace it.

The 6 - Create 6 actions to take next. I say 6 because too many actions can be overwhelming, which inhibits you from starting to achieve this goal in the first place. A busy person with 26 additional actions is bound to become overwhelmed. Equally, 1 or 2 actions do not create the required momentum and sense of progress one needs to persist in their goals. The action level is the critical place to focus. Consistently acting will mean you are continually moving in the direction of your sub-goals which are ultimately moving you in the direction of your SMUUT goal (the 1). When I think of a goal related action in my daily mind-cleanse (see GiFT18) it is one that I star because it then gets priority in my daily activity. It provides the discipline we all need to act.

This is a fluid process; every time you take an action, replace it with another. Your first actions can include creating a vision board and other visuals (if you haven't done that already). Other immediate actions can include writing the goal down as clearly as you can, sharing it with key people to create a supportive network that will hold you accountable, or picking a song that helps you think about the goal daily (and playing it on repeat). Other immediate actions can include allocating *Mozart time* to focus on what you need to do to move closer to this goal. These are *set-up* actions. They prepare your arena for you to take actions that are going to move you toward your goal.

If your goal is to run your first marathon, you need to complete these *set-up* actions, but sometime soon, you need to actually start running.

In this way, a big SMUUT goal becomes small. It is about the daily discipline to take and replace actions.

Here is an example of how I use 1+3+6 process. This is the start of a process hence some of the sub-goals and actions are basic. Once you take the actions and achieve the sub-goals you can increase the difficulty as you build towards your SMUUT goal.

In writing this book, I have decided to complete my 2nd marathon, 15 years after my first.

The 1: Run a marathon by the end of 20xx.

The 3: These sub-goals are within reach as I want to build my confidence and create some momentum.

    a. One 10km run within the next 7 days

    b. A minimum 10,000 steps per day for the next 7 days

    c. Zero alcohol for the next two weeks

The 6: Again, these actions are about getting started and putting some building blocks in place:

    a. Research marathons for November/December next year

b. Agree travel plans for next year with Leona (need to be in the right place at the right time and no big holidays in the month pre the marathon)

c. Enter a half marathon for May/June next year

d. Ask Leona to be an accountability partner

e. Ask my son Tom to be an accountability partner – see the next two GiFTs!

f. Go for a 45-minute run today

I asked friends and #futureyou members Gary Duncan and Ian Johnson to share how the 1+3+6 process works for them. Gary's example is from the world of project management (to show the versatility of the process):

'The first time I heard Andy Fell talk about his 1-3-6 goal setting framework, I immediately loved the concept. Having goals is great but sometimes they can seem a long way away, so breaking them down into sub goals and the actions required to get you to where you want to be is a simple and effective way of achieving them.

Andy of course talks about 1-3-6 mainly in the context of personal development. It's a practical tool to get you from where you are today, to where you want to be in the future. I have also found that this framework works equally as well in project delivery and it was the absolute foundation of one of my most recent career successes.

To set the background, I was asked to design, deliver, and embed a new simplified product development framework that would consistently deliver good customer outcomes and make things easier for all stakeholders involved in this process. Led by myself, I formed a small cross functional working group to deliver the project. Having given myself time and space to think through the best approach, I decided to use 1-3-6 and therefore set about communicating with the team how I believed it would work.

I explained the framework to the group as follows:

1 Goal – To deliver the new framework

3 Sub-goals :

1. To write a new policy that would be the foundation of the framework;

2. To create a new template that would be customer focused and simplify the risk assessment process;

3. To introduce a new annual product review process.

6 Next Best Actions – I started with the first six actions that would get us going and build momentum. Two each for the sub-goals and then as we delivered an action, we would replace it with another action and so on, and so on.

The group loved the framework, and off we went, everyone playing their part until the framework was designed, approved, and delivered – a fantastic success that was recognised widely across our business.

Coming back to Andy for a second, he is a firm believer that 'winners debrief more than the average' and that was a vital part of our success, both at a local level and getting buy in from senior stakeholders every step of the way. I also built in an annual review to make sure that the debrief process is ongoing.

So go on, give 1-3-6 a try and you too can be successful in your delivery of excellence in your professional and personal life! '

Now Ian:

'I started using the 136 framework back in January following Andy's #whatwinnersdo blast off event as I liked the simple but effective framework it gave me. The blast off event gave me the initial push and used it to set my SMUUT goal being the 1 in the 136 and then broke this down into the 3 smaller goals and the 6 next actions I need to do.

Initially I got the momentum going by setting one SMUUT goal but found it as a good framework and I have now introduced more SMUUT goals both personal and business related which I review each week.

Once I have set the initial 136 I then communicate it to several others so I am accountable which subsequently makes me more committed to making sure I achieve it.

Personally, I like the fact that if you just set a big goal this often looks a long way off from your start point and can phase you so by breaking it down into 3 sub goals I find this keeps me focused on goals you can achieve in the short term and then the 6 actions look at what you can be doing today.

#136

#decidecommitdo'

Now it's your turn:

1 SMUUT goal:

a)

3 Sub or milestone goals:

a)

b)

c)

6 next best actions:

a)

b)

c)

d)

e)

f)

Remember, every time you take an action, you replace it. Every time you achieve a sub/milestone goal you replace it.

9) Tom's lamp-post GiFT – the power of breaking down your goals, part 2

My son Tom decided to record a #giftbite *.

It was a new venture for him. Determined, he prepared his set-up actions to ensure he spoke to the best of his ability, and he delivered great value. The resulting video offered great advice for those looking to break down their SMUUT goals and move beyond the messy middle.

Whilst neither of us look like natural runners, Tom and I have developed a passion for it and frequently update each other with our new lifetime bests for 5km, 10km, and half marathons, thus making us accountability partners.

Tom is also committed to being a force for good and helping others, with men's mental health being his primary area of interest. His #giftbite was focused on how he decided to run a half marathon while raising funds for his chosen men's mental health charity in the UK.

First, up until this point in his life, Tom had never run that far. The charitable cause provided a focus for his training and an emotional anchor for his goal. Tom put the distance to the back of his mind and focused on the next lamppost and then the next lamppost and then the next lamppost, and so on. In this way, he made his SMUUT goal appear small. Before he knew it, he finished his half marathon and more than achieved the funds he had set out to raise for his chosen charity.

This is a classic way to bring the 1+3+6 method to life. Set the big goal and then the sub-goals, but after you do so, focus on the next best actions (the lampposts). Thinking that you're tired and have 10km left to run can make the mind and body weary, whereas thinking of the next lamppost is energizing and possible.

Whatever goal you are focused on, you can use this thinking to break-down the goal into a series of lampposts. By that, I mean use countdown or count-up charts. If you want to lose a certain amount of weight, create a countdown board. If you need to make 100 sales, create a countdown board. If you are running an event and want to sell 60 tickets, create a countdown or count up board from 60-1 or 1-60.

Once you start crossing these mini goals off, you create energy and momentum.

To summarise the four key points of this GiFT:

1. Create an emotional connection regarding your SMUUT goal

2. Break the goal down into achievable next steps

3. Although, not specifically mentioned in the #giftbite, find an accountability partner (at least one). The charity played that role in this instance.

4. Use countdown or count up boards to create your own series of lampposts.

*#giftbites are short, sharp videos that support my writing and other work and can be found on my YouTube channel (Andy Fell, GiFT631). It is a great way to support the content in this book and often when you see and hear me talk about the GiFTs it will help you deepen and embed your learnings.

10) Tom's GiFT – his ongoing story in his own words.

At the end of his #giftbite, Tom mentions his next goal – to complete a full marathon. I asked him to share his story, both the before and the after the lamp-post story. Here it is, in his own words:

'When I was around 10, my primary school hosted cross country races around some of the village fields. I hated them with a burning passion. So much so that the only way I could be persuaded to take part, was bribery. If I promised my mum that I would keep going and not stop, there was chocolate in it for me. In the decade and a bit since then, running, and now triathlon, have become an integral part of my life. In the time it's taken to get from one end of the spectrum to the other, from bribery to getting up pre-dawn for bike rides, I have learned a lot about myself, and life in general.

My first baby step down the path to where I am today, was in late 2015. I ran a 10k for charity - and I went into it with minimal training. I really didn't enjoy the training, but the charity meant a lot to me, and so it was essentially boiled down to gritting my teeth and getting through it. I crossed the line in 1:02, and suddenly was hit with a wave of euphoria. I'd raised over £700 for charity and had crossed the finish line. Instantly wanting more of that feeling, there and then I declared that I *would* be doing a half marathon next, to raise more money for charity. I didn't want to ask people to donate again for the same distance.

It took just under two years, and a rather long hiatus from running - but I did it! The Great Birmingham Run, 2017. I limped over the line with plantar fasciitis in 2:07. Despite the surprisingly crippling amount of pain, I was once again awash with euphoria. This time, however, my lack of training had an effect, and I was limping around for the next few days. It's safe to say that it put me off running for a while. However, I had surprised myself as I had the resolve to keep pushing through that pain and making it to the end. Between that and having raised over a £1,000 for another charity, it remains one of the proudest days of my life.

So, is that why I still run, for that finish line feeling? Not at all. I just hadn't really started yet. I was only running for the external satisfaction of the fundraising. Whilst great motivation, it didn't allow me to fall in love with the process. When I didn't have a race booked, that motivation suddenly fell to zero.

But that was all soon to change.

Just before moving to university, I wanted to lose a bit of weight as I was feeling uncomfortable in my own skin. So, after about six months away from running I decided that I should go get myself some new shoes and get back into it.

This was helped by a trip out to Australia - the competition between me and dad on treadmill speeds was fierce, and fiercer still when we were out on roads. He was leaps and bounds ahead of me, but I regularly could out sprint him and boy did that feel good. More than that though, I started to feel like I was working on myself, and it felt like the first time ever I had done that. I recorded a #giftbite , talking about how I had finished that half marathon, breaking down a big race into manageable chunks, and how I crossed the finish line by just getting to the next lamppost. And the next lamppost. And then the one after. Until eventually I had crossed that line. This was clearly a message that could be applied to life outside of running: but I was only just realizing it for myself.

Before I knew it, summer was over, and it was the start of a new epoch of my life. University was the making of me. It molded me into the person I am today, and I am so proud of the time I spent there. However, there was a steep learning curve, and I spent a lot of my time outside of my comfort zone, especially at the start. I felt swamped by new responsibilities, pressure to perform well both academically and socially. I found solace in running. It allowed me to focus solely on one thing, to the point where all those other voices in the back of my mind faded away. It felt peaceful, and I was starting to take other lessons from the experiences I was having with running. I realized that running is not the only thing where if you consistently put time and effort in, you'll get rewarded. I learned that with running, and with my academic and social pursuits that it wasn't about having one star workout, one big library 'all-nighter' or a crazy night out that was going to get me fit, a first-class degree, and a solid base of friends. It was the consistent, day in day out effort that would get me to where I wanted to be. Sometimes runs, or exams, or social events didn't go to plan - but I learned that that was okay. I wasn't failing because one session wasn't perfect, it was just a bump in the road.

Though I was loving running throughout that year, I wanted to feel that finish line feeling again, and I felt like I had some unfinished business with the half marathon. So together a friend and I entered the Great Bristol Run, and in September 2019, a year after starting University, I smashed my personal best by 10 minutes. I finished strong too - no limping this time. But getting to that finish line felt like so much more than that. Over that year, I had gained more confidence than I could have possibly imagined. I lost a substantial amount of weight and realized that I was capable of much more than I previously thought. I learned how to deal with stressful emotional situations more positively. I had found that no matter what was going on in my head, a run could make me feel better.

The next real shift in my relationship with exercise came about six months later. Whilst I still ran in that period, my focus was heavily on tennis as I had made the university team.

But then the pandemic happened, and it upturned everyone's life. Suddenly, I was away from my friends, my hobbies, and left listless amidst massive amounts of global chaos. Once again, I turned to running to distract me from the turbulence of the world. Though this time, there was no tennis to also be considering, and so I really could dedicate myself to it.

I was fortunate to have found a silver lining in that huge storm cloud. Running gave me time away from social media, away from the news, with just myself for company. My runs got longer, my thoughts more introspective, and I learned more and more about myself every day. I learned what I didn't miss in the slightest, and wasn't worth re-incorporating into my life, and I learned what I really struggled without. I also got a *lot* better at running and it gave me the feeling that I was still doing something productive with this chaotic time.

I moved back up to Lancaster and truly fell in love with the city. Despite the two years living there, I really hadn't seen that much of it.

During one run around this historic city, I signed up to my first marathon. All the lessons I had learned through running were only proven true by this experience. By consistently chipping away at my goals, and breaking them down into little chunks, I was capable of more than I thought possible.

But it wasn't an easy ride. My intended race got cancelled due to COVID, but I was adamant I would go for it alone around Lancaster. I was fitter than I thought I ever could be, I'd pushed through hard workouts and three-hour long training runs. Then the day finally rolled around. It was July and it turned into the hottest day of 2021, and I tried to run a marathon, on my own, thankfully with my girlfriend cycling next to me for the second half. I struggled through about two and half hours... and I got heatstroke. I was devastated as I thought I was as prepared as I could possibly be.

Since then, this has become another life lesson: sometimes things just don't go your way, and there's nothing you can do to stop it. All you can do is get back on your feet and keep trying.

Thanks to three factors, I managed to do just that.

Firstly, the incredible people I have around me pulled me up, dusted me off, and told me that I needed to carry on and not give up.

Secondly, a marathon I had entered the previous October had been postponed, and I had another chance coming in a few months.

Finally, a few months prior, Sol, one of my greatest friends since I was two years old, discovered cycling.

Shortly after my heartbreak of a DNF, Sol and I had both recently got our new bikes, and thus we set one goal for that summer: getting out on two wheels and seeing as much of our local area as possible. It was glorious. I began to fall in love with cycling the way I had with running. I relished how you could spend much more time in the saddle, go much further, and see so much more.

Before I knew it, summer was over. It was October and marathon time. Was I a better runner back in July? Almost undoubtedly. But as I walked up to the start line, I was mentally more prepared for the effort ahead. I was excited, I knew what I had to do, and felt confident that I could.

I want to keep this as more of a series of lessons from running than a race report, so I'll avoid the details, but I came, I saw, I conquered. I pushed through hard times and finished absolutely elated with a 3:44. I had been conservative but was still over the moon with my time. And I had learned another valuable lesson from succeeding where I had previously failed, and not just about the power of community, or the weather. I had learned that so much of what holds me back is in my head, the way I talk to myself and my confidence - and often has nothing to do with how prepared my body is.

Three weeks later I raced the Lancaster half marathon, having signed up to a pacemaker for a friend who could no longer make it. I went in with no expectations, other than having fun. I came out with a 1:30:56, somehow, and had indeed had a whole lot of fun. Again: it all came down to the mindset I went in with.

The marathon marked the start of my final year at university. After a year of doing it all from my bedroom I wanted to go out with a bang. I joined the running club and found a community of incredible people. I raced cross country races with a smile on my face - and occasionally gritting my teeth through intense pain - and hugged friends on the finish lines. It was a totally new experience, and one that I'll forever treasure, despite the mud. It felt like I'd come full circle from being bribed just to not stop in cross country races all those years ago.

I also started to make the most of living a ten-minute walk away from a fantastic gym and swimming pool. That previous summer when Sol and I had been riding our days away, I was asked the question: "You run. You've started cycling. When you were 9 you were a good swimmer. When are you going to start triathlon?".

Triathlon takes what I love about running, and just gives me more of it. So, on a whim, I went looking for the coolest race that was going on in September 2022 - just before I would start work.

"When will I have this much time to train again?", I thought. So, I signed up to Outlaw Half Bowood.

1.9km Swim, 90km Bike, 21.1km Run on a brutal course.

I knew that with dedication, consistency, and just having fun with it, I could do it.

I signed up for an Olympic distance triathlon in Windermere as an exam finishing present to myself in July - almost exactly a year after my failed marathon attempt. It would also help my preparation for the Outlaw Half. This time however, it was a different story. I ended up finishing 22nd overall out of 170 and having the time of my life. The camaraderie checking into transition at 5am was an unspeakably beautiful feeling.

I truly love all three sports, both in training and racing. I have always relished being in the water from a young age, and the repetition of pool swimming allows my mind to wander and ponder, decompress and theorize.

Cycling has given me some of the greatest days out with friends I've ever had. It's given me gorgeous views, and there are few things like the satisfaction of cresting a brutal hill climb.

Running has changed my life. It's taught me so much about myself, as well as how to be a better me: how to deal with setbacks, how to grow and how to accomplish great things. It's also given me confidence in my own ability and deep, meaningful, and truly connecting conversations with friends.

This all culminates in September 2022. Outlaw Half Bowood. Known as the "most challenging but charming" course on the Outlaw calendar, it was the biggest physical and mental test I had put myself through. But I had come too far to spend the whole race fearful of it not going to plan. Instead, it was a celebration of the end of my time at university, it was a celebration of who I've become, and how I've grown. That's not to say it was easy - it was a rollercoaster, and I felt both agony and euphoria at different points of the race. What is much more important than the fact that I finished, or that I blew my target time out of the water, is the journey that got me there, a journey that I'm still on.

I love Brandon Sanderson's books, and so I want to end with a quote from one. Whilst this has been a love letter from me to exercise, I hope it shows that by learning about yourself and finding something you love you can change your life. And most importantly, have a lot of fun on the way.

Here's the quote:

"And so, does the destination matter? Or is it the path we take? I declare that no accomplishment has substance nearly as great as the road used to achieve it. We are not creatures of destinations. It is the journey that shapes us. Our call used feet, our backs strong from carrying the weight of our travels, our eyes open with the fresh delight of experiences lived."

11) The GiFT from the email

Tom's story is about so much more than the exercise, the running, and the triathlons. It is about setting and re-setting SMUUT goals, dealing with setbacks, learning about yourself and using movement to create a strong, positive and healthy mindset. It is about finding and following a passion and doing more of what you love which benefits all aspects of your life. I also learnt a powerful life lesson from my own running experience.

In 2008, I decided to run the Edinburgh marathon to raise money for the Children's Hospice Association of Scotland. Children's charities were close to the heart of our close friend Caroline McFarlan, and to my colleague, Audrey, whose daughter, Rebecca, is in a wheelchair. Both are role models for living with optimism, persistence, and resilience.

I trained hard for this marathon and changed my approach to hydration, food, and alcohol consumption. Considering that the race was in May, the primary training months were in the Scottish winter and early spring. I often slipped on black ice or was pelted by freezing rain while heading out in the dark, cold early mornings for my pre-work runs. But I was dedicated.

The Sunday before the race, I went for my last run before tapering down the training. After about a mile, I stopped. I had a cold and was struggling to breathe. I trudged home a little despondent and spent the next week in the sauna, hoping to sweat out the cold.

On the following Friday night, just two days before the marathon, I stood in my kitchen with a towel over my head and my head over a bowl of steaming water laced with eucalyptus oil. I slipped into a victim mindset (see the next section). I felt sorry for myself and adopted a *'poor me'* mentality. I sent Audrey a text telling her that "it's not fair" after all the "sacrifices" I had made.

Audrey responded almost immediately. Her words shocked me out of my victim mindset, and changed my state instantly, making me focus on what mattered most—raising money for those less fortunate than myself. It was a big wake-up call.

The real goal was to raise as much money as possible. It did not matter if I ran, walked, or even crawled. What mattered most—in Audrey's words—were "the looks on the faces of those kids at CHAS when we presented the cheque." This created a deep emotional connection to the goal and an image to carry with me in my mind.

The marathon surely became difficult after 20 miles. I struggled with cramps and a total lack of energy. Finally, a fellow runner came alongside me and ran with me until I got back into some kind of rhythm. He was the wind beneath my wings.

After he moved ahead of me, I returned Audrey's email to my head. I saw the kid's faces in my mind, thus demonstrating the power of a clear emotional connection to a goal linked to visualisation. Being able to see in your mind WHY you are doing what you are doing gives you greater strength and resilience.

I finished. It took longer than I expected or wanted, but it didn't matter. We raised almost £20,000 and made a difference. I keep Audrey's email with me and refer to it often. It is a constant reminder to be appreciative of what I have rather than waste time feeling sorry for myself, complaining, or living with a negative mindset. It continues to change my state and fire me into action many years later.

12) The GiFT from the stage – a practical exercise to bring a SMUUT goal to life.

Some people find creating a SMUUT goal straight forward. It is something that has sat at the back of their mind for a period and when they give themselves the time and space to think about it, everything falls into place quickly. For others, they need a little more help to kick-start their journey. The following exercise which is part visualisation and part practical helps.

Take your time with this exercise. It gives you the opportunity to be creative, have some fun, think big and then get a lot more practical and into the detail. It will give you actions for your 1+3+6 list as well as getting you to consider what you need to change or just stop to create some time and lose non helpful activities.

Complete the exercise as we go:

1. Pick a date and imagine yourself on a stage collecting the award of your choice. It is something meaningful (but it does not need to be an actual award like an Oscar or a gold medal). Examples could be the "best new leader in x company"; "the top sales advisor in x company"; "the best netball coach in the region"; "the most supportive mentor in the industry"; "the top student in ancient history" or "the most environmentally aware leader

in the community." These awards may or may not exist. What matters is that they provide you with a centre of focus.

Date:

Award you are collecting:

Visual representation you can create for your vision board:

2. Visualise the awards ceremony—the room, the lighting, the stage, the backdrop, and the vibe. Picture someone on stage who is the person announcing the award winner. This is someone you know well and see often. You want that person to become another goal-trigger, where every time you see them, you think of the goal.

   Venue:

   Person on stage:

3. Your name is called out and as you head to the stage, that person tells the audience about your achievements and why you deserve the award you've won. Write this speech down here or in your journal to embed it in your mind. By writing it, it also gives you a sense of what you need to do to receive the award and deepens the connection to the goal. Keep the speech with you and reread it frequently. Keep it short and punchy:

Award announcers' speech: (start by writing, 'your name here' won this award because (s)he.......... As in Bill won this award because he......)

....

....

....

....

....

....

....

....

4. It is now your turn to give your acceptance speech. Make sure you capture how you feel to create an emotional connection. List the people who helped you achieve the goal and what they did to help you. This can include speeches you find inspiring, books that really helped you as well as people in your network.

Start by writing: 'I am delighted to have won this award. I feel amazing and it is one of the proudest days of my life. I want to th ank...,'

5. Any goal orientated visualizations are powerful. Add as many extra touches as you want. Hear the song you'll walk across the stage to, and the outfit you'll wear as you do so. Try to be as detailed as possible. Add a picture of the outfit to your vision board. This will help excite and motivate you.

Song:

Outfit:

Once you have completed this creative, energising, and visual part of the exercise, it is time to get practical. When you are ready, complete the questions and actions as follows. Take your time and think it through. The first response may not always be the best response.

1) To be on that stage and win that award, what do I need to start doing?

1. ....

2. ....

3. ....

2) To be on that stage and win that award, what do I need to stop doing? (i.e., what activities can I stop to create capacity for actions that serve me better? What is getting in the way, wasting time and energy?) Do you watch too much content via your television or spend too long scrolling through social media or playing games on your phone or desk-top? Do you feel tired because you over-eat or drink during the week? For some activities, it may be reducing as opposed to stopping completely.

1. ....

2. ....

3. ....

3) To be on the stage and win that award, what do I need to continue doing?

1. ....

2. ....

3. ....

4) To be on that stage and win that award, what do I need to do more of?

1. ....

2. ....

3. ....

5) To be on that stage and win that award, what do I need to do differently? This relates to an activity that supports you moving in the direction of achieving your goal and being on that stage. It intuitively feels right but you are yet to get the results you want.

1. ....

2. ....

3. ....

6) To be on that stage and win that award, who's help do I need and why? Go back to your acceptance speech. Who did you name and why?

1. ....

2. ....

3. ....

Make sure you create an action to go and speak to the person(s) to ask for their help!

This exercise sets you up for success. It enables you to have some fun, whilst also working through some of the basic things you need to do to get moving. The critical question is asking what we need to do to keep going and how we can create additional support to maintain our motivation during the messy middle.

13) The GiFT from the Climb – the power of music!

Let's dive into a few more practical examples of areas I mentioned during the previous goal setting GiFT. Let's start with the power of music.

My wife, Leona, set her mind on achieving a massive SMUUT goal. In addition to all the countdown boards, visualization exercises and visual representations she had strategically placed around the house, she picked her goal song, "The Climb" by Miley Cyrus. This was a positive trigger for her, as every time she heard the song, it triggered an association with the goal. She would play the song numerous times during the day.

That being said, it is important to choose a song where the words have meaning or you associate the song with previous successes or when you were at your happiest or best. Picking a song you like without meaning or association will bring enjoyment but might not trigger goal-related actions.

When you play your chosen song repeatedly, it could drive those around you crazy, which will in turn draw them into your goal journey, making them want to help you finish the climb and reach the summit (the goal).

In Leona's case, the rest of the family did everything we could to help so we didn't need to hear the song again! We knew when she was about to devote time to the SMUUT goal within seconds as we heard the opening bars to 'The Climb.'

Along with all the other goal achieving techniques, a strong mindset, and action, Leona thankfully achieved her SMUUT goal.

Actions for you:

1) Spend a maximum of 10 minutes thinking of different songs that you love and have lyrics full of meaning and/or inspiration. Avoid overthinking as you can refine the list later.

Capture as many as you can here:

a) ....

b) ....

c) ....

d) ....

e) ....

f) ....

g) ....

h) ....

i) ....

j) ....

k) ....

Feel free to complete the alphabet with songs if you are in the zone!

2) If you love your music create a new playlist entitled something like 'goal smashing songs.'

3) Identify one song from the list:

4) Put a reminder in your phone at a set time – when you see or hear this reminder, play the song until it becomes a habit. Do it when you have time to focus on the goal.

5) Listen to or google the lyrics. Write out 2/3 of your favourite lines here:

6) Add these lyrics to your vision board and/or carry them with you. I read a great deal. I created a bookmark out of the lyrics of one of my songs so every time I open a book, I am instantly reminded of the lyrics, the song and a need to stay focused on my SMUUT goal. This is just one way to create a visual reminder.

14) The dashboard GiFT – the power of visual reminders

Early in my sales leadership career, I worked with some great financial planners. They knew more about sales and managing sales than I did, and I wanted to learn, copy, and add my own 10% to what I saw them saying and doing.

One morning, Dave, a highly successful planner and sales leader, pulled up at my house in his shiny, top of the range, black BMW. The interior was impressive, with its black leather seats and wood panelled dashboard. I was drawn to the dashboard, not because of its flashy instrument panel, but because there was a picture cut from a travel magazine and pasted on the dashboard above the gear stick. It was an image of a beautiful beach in the Caribbean with golden sand and crystal-clear water.

"Dave, why on earth is that stuck on here?" I asked incredulously.

"Well, Andy, that's where I'm spending my next bonus," he replied. It's important to note that he had yet to earn or even come close to earning this bonus. "That is the first thing I see every morning when I leave the house. I look at it and say, 'Today is going to be the best day I have ever had'."

I realised this was Dave's visual trigger to get him into the zone—his ideal performance state. It was part of his morning routine to look at the beach scene and repeat those words to himself. It fuelled his inner champion and set a positive, action orientated tone for the day. Whatever was going on in his life, he knew he needed to be at his best when he left home to see clients and lead his team.

From that moment, I decided on two things:

1) I needed to spend more time with aspirational people like Dave, and

2) I needed to surround myself with 'dashboards and trophies.'

The trophies were things I had already achieved in life—physical things I could look at to remind myself of previous successes. Not wanting to purely reflect on past glories, the dashboards were things yet to be achieved. It was my equivalent of what Dave had stuck to his own dashboard. Over time, this developed into pictures posted on the fridge, stuck in my journal, and pinned on the walls in my office. The vision board followed.

It's amazing how a picture cut from a magazine started an entire personal goal motivation system.

Questions for you:

Have you created your vision board yet?

What's on it?

Has the recent series of GiFTs prompted further thoughts of what you can add? Everything from song lyrics to the speech about why you won the award.

What other visual reminders can you collect, be they from past achievements or future successes?

Where can you put them, so you see them as often as possible?

15) The GiFT of personal bests

Most of the GiFTs in this book relate to setting goals for ourselves. However, there is one GiFT that can applies to the teams that we lead, people we coach, and family members. Some people are yet to develop a high level of self-confidence and belief so they may not be ready to set SMUUT goals. After working around Dave and his colleague Peter, I was ready to take on the world, but I soon realised that not everyone was in the same position.

When I have the privilege and pleasure to run teams, I expect every person to go a little further than they have before. Imagine a team environment where 200 people are all focused on achieving a new personal best rather than comparing themselves to other team members and colleagues. This builds morale, individual and collective confidence, and enables leaders to find multiple opportunities to recognise, praise, and celebrate their team. This is similar to setting and passing a series of lampposts, one at a time

When I started in sales. I heard expressions like, "First is first and second is nowhere" and "First is first and second is the first loser".

Throw away this type of bravado, as it negatively impacts the majority of people on the team. Imagine you lead 200 salespeople. You stand on stage at the company conference and state, "Laura is number one; she is a winner. The other 199 of you are all losers."

Statements like this are incredibly damaging to people's confidence. While this is evidently an exaggeration and people are rarely that blunt, the essence of the message often gets through to people so they FEEL like losers. This creates a negative spiral of a loss of confidence and self-doubt which further impacts on performance.

In this same scenario, we can recognise those who come first AND those who improve their personal best. Not everyone can come first but everyone can WIN. By acknowledging all those who achieve a new best, it rewards many team members and over time improves the team's collective performance. It also broadens the base of those from whom we can learn. Instead of just the number one person being asked to go on stage and share what they are doing, there are many more opportunities for people to share how they've exceeded their previous achievements. This allows people's mindsets to shift from, "I can't be number one because..." to "I am aiming for a new personal best and I believe I can achieve it because..."

Success breeds success. It is contagious, and as the team culture develops, people become the wind beneath each other's wings in the sense that team members will help and cheer on other team members.

Questions for you:

What approach to goal setting do you take?

Does it differ between what you expect from yourself and how you approach it with others?

How can you collect and understand people's current personal bests?

How can you create a system to praise, recognise and celebrate others as they achieve a new personal best?

What about when people around you achieve a new personal best or a SMUUT goal? What happens then?

16) The GiFT from the Summit!

Walking in the hills of the English Lake District, Jonathan Stevens, a friend and business coach, remarked, "Do you know the summit is NOT the highest point?"

If the walk hadn't been so strenuous, I would have fallen about laughing. I looked at him with a wry smile and said, "Of course it is."

For years afterwards, every time I saw Jonathan, I laughed and joked about his comment that day. Then, during Mozart time, I reflected on this conversation. I started to ask myself whether he was actually right. I wondered, "Is the summit really the highest point?"

I thought about it in the context of goals and how many people stop, celebrate, and then struggle to find the motivation to begin again. Complacency sets in and people drift.

This famous Nelson Mandela passage from *The Long Walk to Freedom* conceptualizes this idea:

> "I have walked that long road to freedom. I have tried not to falter; I have made missteps along the way. But I have discovered the secret that after climbing a great hill, one only finds that there are many more hills to climb. I have taken a moment here to rest, to steal a view of the glorious vista that surrounds me, to look back on the distance I have come. But I can rest only for a moment, for with freedom comes responsibilities, and I dare not linger, for my long walk is not yet ended."

Jonathan was right. It is important to take the time to celebrate and enjoy the view from the summit of a goal achieved. However, you must then set the next SMUUT goal. Rather than stare at the next summit in the far-off distance and realize how much more daunting it is to climb, focus on breaking it down, getting clarity of actions needed to arrive at your destination, and then take the next step.

Here is my approach:

1. Take a moment to celebrate your success.

2. Relook at your vision board, your bucket-list or your desired future state (#futureyou).

3. Take some Mozart time to access where you are in life and what matters most.

4. Journal on potential next SMUUT goals.

5. When you have clarity of goal, re-start a new 1+3+6 process.

6. Use as many of the goal reinforcing techniques as you can to help you through the messy middle.

7. Select an accountability partner or two and go public with the goal.

8. Act. The only way to restart is to restart!

17) The goal setting GiFTs at speed!

This section has provided techniques and frameworks to help you set and move in the direction of your goals. Some overlap with other parts of the success formula as they link to your mindset and the constant need to act. The next sections will go deeper into these areas.

To provide a rapid-fire summary of this section, here are 10 steps to success.

Keep this as a checklist and feel free to add and/or amend it to help you on your next climb.

1. Write your goal down. Repeat this step daily.

2. Challenge yourself. Ask yourself: How committed am I to achieving this goal? Have I set a SMUUT goal to stretch myself and make noticeable progress in my life? If you are not fully committed and if there is no stretch, reassess your goal.

3. Share the goal with members of your winning circle* and friends who will support, challenge, and encourage you. Once your

confidence grows and your belief system is strong, think about sharing your goals publicly. This will focus your mind.

4. Set up an accountability partner. Establish a simple system to keep them updated with your progress. For example, each week, send them a short-written update on your progress. Expect and encourage them to challenge your activity and progress.

5. Pick a song and link it to the goal. Play the song daily or hourly, even. Ensure you love the song and choose one with meaning. If you love music, also create a goal-smashing playlist.

6. Create visual representations of the goal. The more the merrier. This could be an image you download or cut from a magazine, a photo, or a drawing you do yourself. Place these images where you will see them regularly. Add them to your vision board.

7. Break the goal down into sub-goals and next best actions (use the 1+3+6 process).

8. Schedule stretches of time that allow you to focus on your goal and act. Have the discipline to stay focused during these times. Avoid distractions. Hide your phone if needed!

9. Set multiple celebration points. Take a moment to celebrate when you achieve them!

10. Start! The only way to start is to start. Ensure you take immediate action and continue to do so daily to make consistent progress in the direction of your goal.

   *A winning circle is a small group of trusted people who provide you energy, feedback and support. They challenge and encourage you. They want you to succeed and be happy. They act as the wind beneath your wings to enable you to soar to new heights.

SECTION 3
MINDSET

We have discussed the first part of the success formula – Goals. Now we need to turn to the second stage, our mindset. As you will see, there is definitely an overlap between the techniques we can use to support us in the achievement of our goals and what we can do to develop and sustain a strong, positive mindset.

A significant percentage of our success is due to what we believe and what we say to ourselves on a regular basis. Early in my career, I was told that if you say you can or you can't you are probably right. When we feel positive, confident, and resilient, we believe anything is possible. The reverse is also true. When we lack these things, our negative self-talk takes over and we want to stay in or at very best close to the entrance of our personal cave.

This section talks through some additional actions we can take to bombard our subconscious mind with positive energy and stimulus. By working through all the GiFTs in the previous sections of this book, we are already well on our way.

Constant self-development and learning from others help us improve our mindset as well as our capability. It fuels our growth as well as our belief system. Journaling enables us to capture these learnings and supports several activities we work through in this section. Many of the goal related GiFTs have a component linked to strengthening our mindset so our self-talk is influenced by our inner champion as opposed to our inner critic. Vision-boards to songs to visual representations on our dashboards and our fridges build a belief in ourselves as well as our goals.

Throughout my life and career, I have thought about the 4 mindsets:

- Player
- Victim
- Cynic
- Spectator

Bits and pieces of each of these mindsets are in all of us. However, the *player* mindset is the only place from which you can consistently live a great life whilst moving toward your goals, dreams, and potential.

Why?

Those who operate with a *victim* mindset continually feel sorry for themselves, believe that life is not fair, and remove blame from themselves. It is always someone else's fault. They take little or no accountability and responsibility. I refer to it as *poor-me* syndrome. Unfortunately, this is a popular mindset. Those with a victim mindset love to find others to mope around with. Avoid these people as they drain your energy and impact your inner champion. They have no intention of leaving their cave and enjoy complaining about how cold and damp it is.

Those with a *cynical* mindset find reasons to explain why things won't work. You hear expressions like "we've tried it before" and "other people have it easier." They usually attribute other people's success to luck. Think back to the story of the number one salesperson. In this scenario, people with a *cynical* mindset are the ones sitting in the audience justifying why what they are hearing won't work for them. They frequently criticise those who have left the cave and are in the uncomfortable stage of learning new behaviours. These people are quick to say, "See, I told you it wouldn't work!"

Those with a *spectator* mindset procrastinate and overthink. They lack courage and are often held back by their inner critic telling them they aren't good enough. People with a spectator mindset lack the confidence to take decisive action, often for fear of being judged by others. They are usually influenced by those with a *victim* or *cynical* mindset. Personal best thinking is a good way to help spectators take baby steps forward until their confidence grows and they move into the player mindset.

Those with a *player* mindset are out of the cave and in the arena looking to move forward toward their goals. They get comfortable with being uncomfortable. They are can-do people with a positive, optimistic, action-orientated, resilient, and persistent belief system. They understand the need to take on new behaviours and live with a growth mindset. When they make a mistake, they learn the lesson and move on.

The following GiFTs are designed to further help us either adopt or maintain the player mindset.

Before we do that, I want you to think about the company you keep.

Why spend time or give space to those who are predominantly living with a *victim*, *cynical*, or *spectator* mindset?

How does it help you move forward?

How does it help you believe in yourself?

How does it help you set and go after SMUUT goals?

How does it help you take a few risks with no guarantee of success?

How does it help you when you stumble and fall?

Do these people lift you up or drag you down?

How does this hinder you from living the life of your dreams?

Look to push all negative influences out of your life.

I recognise this can be difficult but as ex-NFL footballer, Trent Shelton, one said, we "need to love (some) people from a distance." People who we cannot exclude from our life but who criticise and damage our confidence and belief system. They have given up on their dreams and want you to do the same. Minimise time with these people where you can.

Instead, look to create a winning circle of people with a positive, can-do, supportive, and uplifting energy. Look for aspirational people who are already living a happy and successful life. Find the right mentors and/or coach. Surround yourself with people who you can trust with your goals and dreams—people who are out of their own cave and making their way to their next summit. People who will give you constructive feedback and challenge you to become the best version of yourself.

The L/C+10% way of thinking is born out of this concept. Seek successful people, teams, and businesses and learn what they do. In life, people with likeminded mindsets tend to gravitate to each other.

The *player* mindset means your inner champion is overpowering your inner critic. In this part of the book, let's discuss the ways in which you can help it succeed in this regard. I deliberately present a range of options all of which are designed to help you improve and strengthen your mindset.

Take your time to work through this section. Please complete the exercises and be willing to stay out of the cave as some require repetition for value to be seen. Complete each GiFT with a player's mindset. Avoid any cynical thoughts like 'I've tried this before' or 'this is not for me.' Give each one a go. At the end of the section, reflect on which ones you believe will help you the most. Start with them and build them into your routine.

18) The GiFT of the 4M routine

As part of the foundation GiFTs, we introduced you to the concept of Mozart time. As you have seen, this has become a core daily habit that has made a huge difference over time. Another lesson, again triggered by a GiFT on my 50th birthday enabled me to integrate Mozart time into what became my 4M morning routine.

On my 50th birthday, Leona GiFTed me a couple of great books. The first was 'On Fire' by John O'Leary and the second was Hal El-rod's 'The Morning Miracle.' I read and reread them both in the six months between that birthday and leaving the corporate world. Both really helped my confidence and reinforced my desire to set up my own business and live life on my terms.

Hal's book shares his morning routine and the profound impact it has made on his life. It really emphasised the importance of winning the start of the day and finding a routine that helps you get into a great mindset. From reading the book, my own morning routine crystallised. I had been undertaking some powerful morning activities, but I had not connected them in a sequence to maximise the benefits of each one individually and the collective routine.

I named it 'The 4M routine' and it consists of 4 activities. Each activity is valuable on its own, however there is an even greater impact when the 4 activities are done in sequence as follows:

Movement

Mind-cleanse

Meditation

Mozart time

The real key in this regard is consistency. It is about the accumulated value over time. It is about creating a winning habit to repeatedly set your day up for success.

Movement: I encourage people to start their day with some simple movement such as a 20 to 30-minute walk. I believe in the connection between a healthy and active body and a healthy, active mind. Moving can fuel creativity and help you think through priorities, problems, and opportunities. It can provide ideal subject matter for Mozart time.

If I am on my own, as I move, I will frequently listen to a podcast to get my daily dose of self-development or run through an affirmation or visualisation exercise, which I discuss later in this section.

Starting everyday with movement ensures you avoid the temptation to dive into your news feed (mainly negative), scroll through social media, or even worse, jump straight into your inbox and start the day by reacting and dealing with other people's priorities.

Mind-cleanse: Once I have set aside time for and completed my movement, I sit with my journal and cleanse my mind, capturing everything that I need to do or that has the potential to distract my thinking. The things I jot down can either be related to my business or my personal life—or both. At first, I perceived it as an extended to-do list, but over time, one key difference emerged. A to-do list is normally random—it lacks priority and contains lots of low value activities. As my mind-cleanse process matured, I started to review the list, starring the high value items—the ones related to clients, family, and the achievement of my goals.

Once I have starred all the high value items, there are two potential options. If the item can be completed quickly, my objective is to complete it that day. These are the activities I will start with once my 4M routine is complete. If the item requires a period longer than a few minutes, I schedule it in my diary. One of my guiding principles is that 'what gets in my diary gets done.'

I do not feel the need to tick off every item listed as part of my mind-cleanse, but I need to tick off or diarise those with a star against them. Always start with the high value items and make time in your diary to do what matters most. At the end of this GiFT, I have provided a blank copy and a second one with a few examples to illustrate the point.

My mind-cleanse ensures I am organized. It ensures I have captured what is on my mind, therefore giving me a sense of priority. Critically, my mind is free from clutter.

Meditation: I complete a short, 10-minute guided practice using the *Calm* application. This centres and relaxes me, as it reduces any tension, anxiety, or pressure. It increases focus, builds concentration, and keeps things in perspective. My meditation purpose is to develop my mental fitness and champion mindset. Prior to adding the mind-cleanse to my routine, I struggled to meditate. I often sat and found myself thinking of what I had to do during the day, consistently distracted by these thoughts as opposed to concentrating on the meditation practice.

What I have learned is the importance of habit-stacking—the value of one core winning habit leading to another to form a powerhouse routine. I recommend you read or listen to *Atomic Habits* by James Clear to understand this concept on a deeper level.

Mozart time: Meditation is the ideal set up for Mozart time. I am centred, relaxed, and full of good energy. The result is my thinking and journaling has more clarity and creativity. It is where and when breakthroughs happen. Remember, greatness requires stillness, and from stillness comes clarity, breakthroughs, innovation, and success. While Mozart time can be a standalone activity and one, I believe is necessary for success, it is even more powerful when combined with the other 3Ms mentioned above. They provide the ideal set up to maximise its impact.

There are three major benefits to the 4M routine. First, it is a way to get into the ideal performance state and to ensure you start each day with a positive, can-do mindset. Secondly, it creates a disciplined start to the day and is a routine that benefits both the mind and body.

Thirdly, it means starting the day on your terms as you undertake high value activities.

THE

4M PROCESS

M OVEMENT

M INDCLEANSE

M EDITATE

M OZART TIME

I have been using and sharing the 4M routine for a number of years. Here are a few thoughts from people who use the process:

Allan Barr:

Benefits/ Flexibility

I used a variation of the 4M routine over the past few years and have found that this can be used when working from my local office or when working away from home and living in a hotel, the key success is the flexibility.

The real challenge for me for me came when COVID arrived and my established morning routine was thrown into chaos with the "office commute" now a one minute walk from bedroom to spare room and the "movement" component of 4M at the gym removed. At this time it was all to easy to get up, make a coffee and then start the working day without any structure. Working with Andy and the wider Future You community I adapted my 4M routine and built it into my working from home schedule by going out for a morning walk / run and taking MOZART time etc prior to logging on to my pc or looking at emails. While the impact of COVID is hopefully a once in a lifetime disruption the key learning for me is that no matter what disruption life throws at us individually or as a society the 4M routine is adaptable and is a key ingredient to setting yourself for winning day after winning day.

How do I recommend you make the 4M routine a winning habit:

Tip 1 – Get an Accountability Buddy and set up regular check ins (I do fortnightly) to discuss and review the past two weeks – discuss what is working, challenges you are facing and most importantly learn from each other – can you add 10% (or even 5%) to set yourself up for a winning day?

Tip 2- Movement in fresh air is key and if you are struggling for motivation (due to bad weather, pressure at work etc) use visualization and imagine how much better you will feel after the activity. For me the tip that made this a non-negotiable every day was "pretend you have a dog" and no matter what the weather or what is on your to do list you are guaranteed to be out the door at least three times a day.

Tip 3 – Be flexible in how you use the 4M routine i.e., the same activities don't need to be done for in the same order for the same duration of time every day. Sometimes a short walk will be ideal for the movement component other days a longer run may be appropriate. With regards to Mozart time, set aside a short period in the morning and then additional time later in the day. The key is to do what works best for you and make it winning habit not just another routine that you feel you have to follow.

Alan Chapman:

Everyone has the potential to be a better version of themselves and the principals and learnings in this book provide great insight and tangible actions how to achieve this.

Andy uses stories and formulas to show you how to think, act and have a champion mindset, from starting the day with his 4M routine to his end of day debrief.

One lesson I embraced many years ago was to follow Andy's habit of spending as much time as possible studying highly successful people across different walks of life, learning from them, copying or adapting them and adding my winning edge ("adding your own 10%").

One such example is the 4M morning routine. I have always been an advocate of it , but, until recently, I have not been as consistent as I wanted to be.

Following redundancy, job searching and successfully securing a new role at the end of 2020/start of 2021 I decided this would change.

So, my additional 10% was to create a simple daily checklist of all the winning habits I was going to action and cross them off when achieved.

I also adapted to make it my 4M +C routine, which came about from listening to an amazing young man called Duku Forè, who shared his story about taking a cold shower every day until he achieved a particular goal. When I heard this I copied and the cold shower became the C.

Both changes made have been fundamental in transforming how I start every day in the ideal performance state.

This routine gives me the time and space in my own thoughts to set up my day and has given me greater focus. It provides momentum and a sense of perspective. It is the time where many of my ideas and next steps have been born and developed.

Manny Martinez:

I have been following the 4M routine for almost two years. My morning routine starts off with physical exercise for 30-45 minutes. Some of the fitness activities (such as walking) allow me to incorporate meditative practices like prayer and self-reflection, it's like doing 2 "Ms" at once! My mind cleanse is broken up into a mini to-do list. As I write down what's on my mind for the day ahead, I write each activity into A (must do today), B (items for tomorrow), and C (actions for end of week, maybe end of month). I spend time in meditation: for me it's silent prayer, reading scripture, and stillness. During the weekdays, I add 10 minutes meditation with breathing to allow my mind to be still and transition into Mozart Time.

My morning Mozart Time consists of writing down reflections and insights from the morning routine. Less structured (unwritten) Mozart Time occurs in the evening, taking time to look back at the day during a walk or before going to bed.

My 4M practice on weekdays runs from 4:30 am to 6:30 am, it's structured and disciplined. By contrast, I wake up by 6:30 am on weekends, and I break up the routine throughout the morning, a little more flexible. The 4M is an investment in myself so I can share the benefits with others during the day.

Iain Wade:

Why?

I have been adapting Andy's teachings over the last 2 years and I would describe them as truly life changing in two important ways

1/ Clarity: Its helped me to develop greater clarity on what matters most both in terms of work, career and life goals with more time focused on my personal development

2/ Wellbeing: It has also helped me through some tough personal moments. When things in life go awry as inevitably happens from time to time, the tools have helped me regain focus and motivation to move forwards. I would use the analogy of squash here. When you play (and find yourself disorientated in the middle of the court)- you are urged to get back to the T. Things like the 4 Ms have helped me get back to the T when I have been mentally and physically struggling.

How?

- As Andy says- the key is to build up the routines gradually rather than trying to do everything at once and then finding your own marginal gains to compliment them. I have been benefitting from mediation for 4/5 years but the 4 Ms helped me put this into context and use it as an opportunity to create clarity as well as promoting wellbeing.

- I use the 4Ms each day. I simply go for a 10/15 min walk round the block listening to a podcast for Movement. I Mind Cleanse (although I find it more useful to do my 'to do list' the night before- this is just to confirm/amend). I meditate using a UK app called Headspace (Calm is just as good) and then I do 5 mins Mozart time. I would describe this Mozart time as more of a daily preview. I use a diary to journal appreciation and things I am looking forward to, daily mantras, affirmations (in relation to an important meeting, presentation that day) and my big 3. I don't do any more 'big thinking' at this time as I am much more of an afternoon/evening person (owl).

- I have booked out 10 mins Mozart time each afternoon around 3.30pm over a coffee (often stepping back to solve work related problems and an hour on a Friday afternoon where I focus on my development/goals specifically). I try to do daily, weekly and monthly reviews where I look at what's gone well, challenges, learnings and big goals next day, week, month. Embedding this rhythm has been challenging (there are still days/weeks when it slips) but I really feel the benefits of following it when I do

Rebecca Ninness on mastering her own 4M routine and then moving onto her (adapted) 1+3+6 routine:

After the 4M routine became a habit in my life it has been an essential start to my day, I worked on the 6 3 1 goal setting method. This kick starts my year, every year. I link it with Andy's visualisation strategies, and before I know it I am kicking butt. My adaptation is I have 6 smaller goals, working my way up to my 3 bigger goals. My 1 big goal gets closer in sight with every action I take. It helps to visualise achieving this often, so I have this as my screensaver. It's amazing what you can achieve by visualising regularly. It played a big part in winning new member of the year in my new business venture.

As you can see, people have invested time to learn these frameworks. Through consistently applying them, different people have started to adapt and add their own 10% to make it their own. This is brilliant. Adapt the 4M process to serve your own needs. Add to it and make the linkages to the other frameworks, habits and routines to develop your own success system so you can 'kick butt' like Rebecca.

I am a strong believer in the power of making these frameworks and processes your own. Only then will you use them with the consistency required to improve your life.

As promised, here is the mind-cleanse I use:

DAILY MIND CLEANSE

	HIGH VALUE ITEMS	
	DO TODAY	SCHEDULE

DAILY MIND CLEANSE - EXAMPLES

	HIGH VALUE ITEMS	
	DO TODAY	SCHEDULE
CONTACT CLIENT X	✳	
WRITE CLIENT PROPOSAL		✓
BOOK RESTAURANT FOR FAMILY DINNER	✳	
WRITE QUARTERLY REPORT		✓

19) Andrew Wilson's GiFT – how I bookend my day with my version of the 4M routine:

In the previous GiFT, we ended with 5 different examples of how the 4M routine is helping different people. To me it is such an important framework to help our mindset and belief system as well as setting up our day/week/month for success I have devoted a chapter to another story of the impact the GiFT631 frameworks can have on your life. This is Andrew's story.

'Back in 2017 I was made redundant as an Area Manager from a large UK bank. I had been there for 15 years; I was very institutionalized. I loved the bank, and it was all I really knew but that chapter closed.

I had to move forward, and I decided to move forward with what I was good at …. Helping people, and more specifically what I was qualified in, mortgage advice.

When I attended my interview at First Mortgage, Ian and Antony asked me "why are you not applying for the Regional Manager position?"

Maybe there was a bit of self-doubt or impostor syndrome with my confidence taking a knock with my exit from my previous role but truthfully, the real reason I was applying for a mortgage adviser position was the exact response I gave "I want to learn the role of being a mortgage adviser in this broker firm and fully understand it before I lead and develop others in that role"

So, it was set, I would join First Mortgage as a Mortgage and Protection adviser.

No problem, yet big problem!!

I have just agreed to a massive pay cut! Coupled with the loss of all the company benefits of working for a big bank such as company car, final salary pension, sick pay, life and critical illness cover, the real cost of the drop in income was far greater than the difference between the two take home pays. Also, I have just signed up to a

2-hour daily commute with the added cost that comes along with that too.

No regrets. I must move forward, and I did not come to this firm to earn a basic salary. I came to help as many people as I can.

One of the first things I did when I settled into First Mortgage was meet with my line manager Amanda Reid and once all the niceties and formalities were out of the way she asked me "how much would you like to earn?". This I had given a lot of thought. Currently I am running my household finances at a deficit. I am married. I'm a father. I must make this work. I could count on my fingers the number of months I had left until I had to dip into my long-term savings.

Without a moment's thought I told her my number.

A number that would help our family achieve our goals, live comfortably and out earn the line manager who let me go from my previous role and turned my world upside down.

Unflinching Amanda said, "let's build a business plan."

Together we worked back from a total earnings figure, to calculate how much business I would have to convert, how much I would have to write, broke it down to a weekly amount based on current peer average and broke it down again to a daily amount. We took it further and looked at the conversion ratio of clients met to clients helped and at the end I had my formula. If I see this many people per day, convert this many to business, help them at this value and if I do that every week, I will achieve my number.

I was clear on what I had to do.

No problem. Well, I say that, but the problem is, it's hard. It's hard to stay consistent. Often, we know what to do, how to do it, why we do it, but doing it... every day ... every week... every month... it takes more than motivation, it takes discipline.

I asked myself "What's the key to discipline?". Then I thought, hang on, I've just literally ran a marathon!! A marathon...! I trained, outdoors, all through the Scottish winter, all through the cold, dark, wet months. I completed my first marathon in May 2017, the Stirling

Marathon and I am proud of my 4 hours 14 mins time. I know it's not going to qualify me for the Boston Marathon any time soon, but it was my marathon, I done it, I made the bold statement to my friends and colleagues, I proved those wrong who scoffed at the cyclist who declared he was going to run a marathon who had previously never travelled further than a mile without wheels, but I done it.

It's consistency, the key to discipline is staying consistent enough to build a habit, a routine. Ah, a routine?! I need a routine.

I developed a routine that helped put me in a player mindset every day. No days off, this was not a Monday to Friday routine, this was every day. I did not want any interference creeping into my mindset. I needed to be at my best so I could give my best and better serve not only my clients, but my family.

My Morning Routine

Wake up – In the morning it is tempting to roll over, grab the phone, switch off the alarm and start scrolling. Don't do that. As tempting as it is, I did not touch my phone other than to switch off the alarm. Furthermore, I disabled all alerts and pings for social apps. It removed the temptation to click the app and get the quick dopamine fix. When I click the app, it's on my terms, I choose when to open it at an allotted time of day and when I am in the right mindset.

Meditate – I go into the bathroom to do my morning meditation. I do this for peace and quiet and privacy, so I was not interrupted. I would start by being grateful. Being grateful for having air in my lungs, food in the cupboards, a safe warm house, an able body, and the ability to think. I am grateful for having a job, a car to get to that job, the ability to earn money and provide for my family and the fact that I have been given a brand-new day, the sun is coming up and it is going to be a good day.

During my meditation I also put good wishes out into the universe. I wish well to my mother, who lives alone as a widow. I wish well to my sister who is trying to have a baby. I wish well to my brother who is trying to buy his first home. I think about the other people I have come across, the goals they have shared with me or their worries and wish them the strength and ability to overcome their challenges.

I then give thanks. I say thank you for the things I don't yet have. The things on my goal list and bucket list, the things I'd like to have, the places I like to go, the people I'd like to meet. I say thank you for having these things as if I have them already. It's as if I am talking on behalf of my future self.

Movement – After my meditation, I get ready to start the day, before I leave the house for work, I take the dogs for a walk. This gives me some head space to start getting geared up for the day, gets the blood pumping and, let's be honest, nothing makes you feel happier than seeing a dog's love for you!

Mind Cleanse – On the way to work, I have a no radio policy in the car. There's no news like bad news and there is no shortage of bad news. Jim Rohn said, "every day, stand guard at the doors of your mind". I would be sure not to fill my head with negativity. I prefer to listen to podcasts such as High Performance or go on You Tube and listen to Jim Rohn or if I want something spiritual Joe Olsteen.

When I arrive in the city for work, I still have a 20-minute walk to the office (remember, I am not rolling in cash yet and if I can save money on city center parking I will. In my eyes, that money saved on parking is almost a family holiday every year, and how much do shoes cost anyway? I'm walking!)

Lists – When I arrive at the office, I am in a good mood and I make the point of saying to all my colleagues "good morning, this is going to be a great day!". It sounds corny, but this is me subliminally saying to my colleagues "I don't want to hear bad news just yet". When I get to my office, I change from my walking shoes to my work shoes. I open the cupboard where I keep them and inside the cupboard door, pinned in clear view is my business plan. The plan I know inside out and therefore doesn't have to be there, but it's there as a constant reminder to keep me accountable for what I must do today. I close the door and look up at the sole photo frame on my desk. My son, smiling at me, another reminder of my why. I smile back at him.

Before I even turn on my PC, I open my notepad and write a list. I will write a list of all the good things I want to achieve today. I plan each day with a bit of wiggle room to allow me to deal with unexpected emergencies.

I then open the emails and skim them to pick out the important ones and add them to my list.

Then I begin my working day.

The morning routine in reverse!

At the end of the day, I ask myself "was today a good day?" "Did I achieve everything I set out to achieve?" "If I was self-employed, would I pay myself a salary for today?"

I then write a list of all the things I want to do tomorrow to make tomorrow a good day. Don't use your head as a filing cabinet, get it on paper, write it down and free up some mental head space for family time.

I look back at the photo of my son and get excited at the thought of finding out how his day went and spending time with him.

I change my shoes and look at my business plan, content with the fact I am on track or aware of any shortfall and what I must do tomorrow.

I begin the walk to the car, every step physically away from the office feels like a step mentally away from the office. Leaving my office worries in the office and being sure not to take these home.

In the car I listen to the same mix of positive energy podcasts, or self-development You Tube clips.

When I get home once all the family duties are done, I make sure I have at least 30 – 60 minutes to do some high intensity exercise or weightlifting. Healthy body, healthy mind.

I limit TV time and certainly no junk TV.

Before bed I go through the same meditation cycle of being grateful, wishing well for others and giving thanks to my future me for all the good that is coming.

No social media at bedtime and certainly no phones in bed. Instead, I would read something non-fictional, something that interests me such as mountaineering, personal endeavor, cycling, personal development and history books.

Days roll into weeks and weeks roll into months and by quarter 3 in my first year in First Mortgage Amanda sat down with me during a 121 and said, "do you know you are on track to hit the 200 club?!" The 200 club is the high achievers club for senior advisers in the firm. Not only was I meeting my business plan, but I was also exceeding it by far.

I didn't think much of it, and I stuck to my daily routine. I know how many customers I must help and if I can stay in the player mindset, I will serve them as best as I can.

At the end of the year, I had exceeded my goal. I achieved the 200-club status in year 1 which is almost unheard of. Not only that, but I also had a great balance in my life. I committed to my son to take karate lessons with him and so 3 days a week we would go to the dojo and work towards our dan grades. This gave me accountability. In an environment where earnings are uncapped and you can work as many hours as you wish, it was important to me to have a reason to leave the office at 17:30 at least 3 nights per week, I am a father after all and when will I ever get these days back if I miss them?

On top of that I studied towards and achieved my level 4 diploma in financial planning which gave me a higher level of knowledge in my industry, this helped me better serve not only my clients but also allowed me to give good counsel to my colleagues too.

I am truly grateful for all the twists and turns life has taken so far, even the hard times which can be hard to swallow. My mum always said; "what's for you will not go by you!" which is true to some extent, but it can seem a bit defeatist.

I prefer the quote from the greatest movie trilogy of all time, and my parting gift to you are the words of Doc Brown "Your future hasn't been written yet. No one's has. Your future is whatever you make it. So, make it a good one!"

20) The screensaver GiFT

After I complete my 4M morning routine I turn on my laptop.

Like Rebecca, I ensure that my laptop's screensaver, at all times, is an image that inspires me. I am sure this related back to what I saw in Dave's black BMW all those years ago. It is something that reminds me to appreciate what I have and inspires me to make the most of the day ahead. It is another GiFT from one of my children.

When my daughter, Lucy, was 12, I asked her to create a screensaver for me. I described what I was looking for, but not how it needed to look exactly. She nailed it and I have kept this screensaver ever since. I strongly recommend you go to my YouTube channel and check out the #giftbite where I show this screensaver and describe it's meaning. It will bring this GiFT to life.

Lucy gave me an image of two people, Bethany Hamilton and Nick Vujicic, surfing on the same board in Hawaii. They are clearly having fun and enjoying what they're doing.

I asked Lucy why she had chosen this image, and she answered:

"Well, Dad, if they can do that, you can do anything!"

Every time I turn on my laptop, I look at the image and I replay these words in my head. It serves as a constant reminder that I can achieve my SMUUT goals and the life of my dreams. This helps me maintain a positive, can-do, action orientated mindset each day. During tough times, this screensaver helps me persevere and stop feeling sorry for myself (as we know the victim mindset, however temporary, does not help in anyway).

For those who don't know Bethany and Nick, you may not understand why the image is so inspiring. At 13, while surfing, Bethany had her arm bitten off by a shark and Nick was born without arms and legs. I have added the screensaver before the questions and actions at the end of this GiFT. I am sure when you see it and watch the #giftbite you will see why I find it so inspiring.

Either one of them could find many reasons to be sitting on the sidelines living with a spectator, victim or cynical mindset while feeling sorry for themselves. Yet they were living life to the fullest—100% in the player zone. They live with a true champions mindset.

In the previous section, we spoke about visuals to support your goals and ideally the creation of your own vision board. Your screensaver will be one of the most frequently seen images in your daily life. Therefore, it is important to create something that's powerful to you.

Be willing to keep changing your screensaver until you find the right image or collection of images. As soon as it loses impact, change it.

Questions for you:

What is your current screensaver? Your phone? Lap-top? Desktop? Other devices?

What does it say to you every time you see it?

Does it inspire you to have a great day and make the most of the opportunities ahead?

Does it trigger a connection to one or more of your goals or bucket-list items?

Actions for you:

Take some Mozart time to think about an image or series of images that you could turn into a screensaver.

You may decide you want more than one to either rotate them or for different devices.

On one device you might want to keep a picture of your partner/family/pets. That's cool!

Upload your chosen images onto your device or devices.

Journal why you chose this image or images and what it means to you. By doing this you are creating a deeper trigger for every time you see the image.

21) The GiFTs of gratitude and appreciation

After I complete my daily 4M routine, I feel focused, organised and centred. I have had time to think and focus on what matters most. I then turn on my laptop and see my screensaver which powers up my belief system and inspires me to recognise that I need to live in the player mindset and go after my SMUUT goals. I feel ready to win the rest of the day.

However, I like to start by expressing gratitude and appreciating what is around me and all I've been given in life.

This stems from my paternal grandad.

Toward the end of his life, grandad lived for a few months each year at 631, the property after which my business is named. He left school at 12, initially working as a stable boy in an English country house, sleeping in the stables with the horses. He then progressed to working in the main house as a footman. He always remembered these humble beginnings.

My recollections of my grandad developed into a belief around living and leading with a servant's heart, which means living with a generous spirit and a mentality that finds and appreciates the good in others. It means respecting everyone regardless of their position, title, and financial standing, remaining humble, and living with gratitude.

The saying I associate most with my grandfather is, "I had no shoes and complained, until I met a man with no feet." I was taught it came from Mahatma Gandhi, although it is widely quoted from a number of different sources dating back to a 13th century Persian poet. Regardless, its meaning is what matters most. This saying urges us to be grateful for and appreciate what we have. It tells us to live with a positive spirit and a sense of optimism. It is another example of a *player* mindset emerging once the trigger of the man with no feet helped the author snap out of the *victim* mindset.

My grandfather told me to "always do people a good turn" and never worry about whether that favour would be repaid. He said, "Just do it because you can."

I follow my 4M routine with an act of appreciation/gratitude for a friend, family member, colleague, client, business partner, or someone who has done even the smallest thing to brighten or improve my world. This might be a text, social media message, phone call, handwritten note, or card. I love putting good feelings out into the universe and believe this simple act creates a ripple that goes beyond what I know and see. It helps my mindset and I know it helps the mindset of others.

I also have space in my #whatwinnersdo journal where I note 2 or 3 things daily that I am happy and grateful for. This takes only a few seconds but always helps me feel good. Imagine if you do this every day for two weeks. After that period, you have a list of at least 25 things you are happy and grateful for, even though some may be repeated more than once. If ever you are having a bad moment, read the list and remind yourself there are so many things to be grateful for.

Let's start your list now. Things to be happy and grateful for:

1. ....

2. ....

3. ....

4. ....

5. ....

6. ....

7. ....

8. ....

9. ....

10. ....

Before moving to the next GiFT think about appreciation. Who do you want to reach out to acknowledge for an act of kindness, friendship, thoughtfulness, or love? Again, note down a few names now and then send them a message of some description before moving onto the next GiFT:

1. ....

2. ....

3. ....

4. ....

5. ....

6. ....

For those leading teams you might want to extend this practice to make an even greater difference to your own mindset but also those around you.

22) The GiFT of saying thank you

Expressing gratitude, sharing praise, and recognizing others was a core morning activity long before GiFT631. One of my early leaders, Mike Jeacock , taught me the value of fun (the most important *F* word in business), along with seeking and seeing the best in people. Mike also shared his belief that every leader could find 15 minutes a day to say thank you.

Being new to leadership at that time, I decided to set aside 15 minutes a day in my diary for this purpose. As with Mozart time and other practices, what gets in my diary gets done. It fitted perfectly with my grandad's philosophy and became a winning habit that I carried with me to every role I took on in both the UK and Australia. Having a personal best approach provides multiple opportunities to say thank you to people, teams, and business units. It spreads praise and recognition more widely and more frequently.

The 15 minutes I set aside to give thanks came in the form of handwritten letters, notes, and cards, which made the act more personal and meaningful. I extended this act to people across different functions in the company I worked for as well as external business and community partners. I felt fantastic writing and sometimes text messaging people (in the early 2000s it was hand-written faxes too!!). The practice originated to help other people's mindset and belief system. It did just as much for my own.

The practice also reinforces the behaviours you love and appreciate as a leader. Other leaders in your business start to see the impact and replicate the behaviour. Recipients of your 'thank yous' share your message with their colleagues which in turn creates more desire to replicate the behaviours across your team. A new tone develops around catching people doing something RIGHT, praise, recognition, and celebration.

Over the years, people have sent me photos of the cards I mailed to them dating all the way back to the 1990s. When times are challenging, it is amazing how many people remember your acts of kindness and gratitude and without asking, do what they can to help.

These seemingly small gestures can make all the difference.

Royston Guest, the CEO of Growth Pathways and a tremendous example of someone who lives in the *player* mindset, talks about "throwing out the positive boomerang." By consistently putting good out into the universe, the positive boomerangs will always come back to help you.

Questions for you:

What, how and when do you recognise great behaviour in others?

What can you do daily to throw the positive boomerang?

Who can you catch doing something RIGHT?

Actions for you:

Schedule a short period of time (even 5 minutes) daily to either say a series of 'thank yous' or to appreciate others as in the previous GiFT.

I still believe in the power of hand-written praise but can recommend Touchnote as a great way to create and send personalised cards.

23) The *Be Amazing* GiFT

What do we do in the moments when we stumble or in the moments when our inner champion is challenged? How do we respond?

Each morning, when I drop my youngest daughter, Lily, off at school, we make eye contact as I mouth, "Be." She replies in the same manner with, "Amazing." I want her to leave the car smiling, with a little burst of confidence, feeling great about herself. The expression, **'be amazing'**, has become a wider catch cry. These simple words have a profound impact and help me, as well as others, get into our ideal performance state.

As part of my daily journaling, I often note down occasions when I am proud of something I have achieved. Some are bigger achievements, while others are small wins. The sheer act of writing them makes me feel great. This has become my own **be amazing** list.

This habit started many years ago after a conversation with friend and ex-colleague, Tim Sims. Tim is a perfectionist and little negatives tend to have a disproportionate impact on his view of what he has achieved.

I once told Tim he should go home thinking about the best things that happened during the day as opposed to the occasional negative things. He came back to me a few days later saying it helped but not enough. He still got drawn to the odd thing that hadn't gone as well as he wanted it to. I suggested he go out and buy a success journal.

"What's that?" he asked.

"Simply buy a notepad, write success journal on the front, and, without exception, write down the best thing you have done each day. Whenever you need to refocus or feel better, pick it up and start reading. Keep reading down the list of these daily successes until you feel great about yourself again."

The last few pages of the #whatwinnersdo journal are dedicated to this practice—a space where you can write down the things you are proud of. What you write is up to you, as it is for your use and benefit. I do, however, encourage you to capture everything—big and small successes. It is your own **be amazing** list to help you feel good, recover from a stumble or fall, and ensure you have the confidence to keep going. It is another quick way to change your state and ensure your mindset remains positive.

Let's start now.

Actions for you:

Create a name for your list. 'My success list' or 'Things I am proud of' or something more creative such as your own version of the 'Be Amazing list.'

Get to a list of 10 things you are proud of as quickly as you can.

Avoid overthinking.

Keep going if you want to. The more you write the better you feel.

Daily, add to the list.

In a moment of self-doubt, get out the list and start reading through it.

Be amazing list (replace with your name):

1. ....
2. ....
3. ....
4. ....
5. ....
6. ....
7. ....
8. ....
9. ....
10. ....

24) The affirmations GiFT

While the **be amazing** list is a powerful state changer, affirmations provide a similar benefit.

I started to consistently use affirmations since I read *The Morning Miracle*. Initially, I wrote a whole series—each one a present tense statement of who I want to be and the life I want to live. To ensure I stay in the present tense, many of my affirmations start with "I am..."

For example, "I am an amazing coach. I am an internationally renowned public speaker. I am a two-time published author. I am enjoying being the CEO of my own life. I am happy and fulfilled by helping other people reach their true potential."

The #whatwinnersdo journal has a section to list as many affirmations as you want and need. It is another way of building a champion mindset and bombarding the subconscious mind in a positive way. Before a big meeting, video conference, telephone call, or presentation, I frequently reread the list as it helps me feel good about who I am and what I am about to do.

I have refined my use of affirmations as time has progressed. I now have a chosen affirmation that I rewrite everyday as part of a daily process, which captures a few of my daily winning habits in a matter of minutes. Repetition of this affirmation builds a more unshakeable belief. It also focuses my actions and reinforces my desired future state whilst helping to overpower my inner critic and any sabotaging thoughts I may have.

My chosen affirmation is as follows: "I am enjoying being the CEO of my own life and the time and financial freedom it brings."

Actions for you:

As with your be amazing list, start to create a list of affirmations.

Start everyone, 'I am.........'

Keep adding to this list

Feel free to repeat ones that resonate with you.

Use this list as a powerful tool to help you focus your activity and strengthen your mindset.

Affirmations. I am...

1. ....
2. ....
3. ....
4. ....
5. ....
6. ....
7. ....
8. ....
9. ....
10. ....

When you are ready to select one chosen affirmation, capture it here:

25) The state changer GiFT

Some days, you may feel as though you are starting to drift, particularly if you're spending too long in meetings or focused on your incoming emails and messages. On other days, things are not going your way or something significant has happened to damage your confidence. Perhaps you have lost your biggest client, the best member of your team has resigned, you miss out on a promotion or a big sale.

How do you recover and pick yourself up quickly?

By contrast you may feel you want to pump some extra air into your tyres as you have a big moment ahead. You want to feel, look and sound confident and self-assured.

What can you do to quickly change your state in these moments?

In this simple, effective, and speedy state changer, I combine the content of some of the GiFTs we have already covered. As always, feel free to learn, copy, adapt, and add your own 10%.

The core steps (60 seconds in total):

1) Write down your primary SMUUT goal (10 seconds)

2) Write down your chosen affirmation (10 seconds)

3) Write down 2 or 3 things you are happy/grateful for (20 seconds)

4) Reread or add to your *be amazing* list (20 seconds)

If time is pressing, just use these 4 core steps.

The self-development step:

5) Watch a #giftbite and note down one thing that resonates with you (120 seconds)

The next best action steps:

6) Write the most important thing you need to do (30 seconds)

7a) If it's quick, do it!

7b) If it requires, times and focus schedule it into your diary for a time when your energy is usually at its best (2 minutes to schedule). Protect that time from other activities.

I add steps 6) and 7) because when you have changed your state and feel great and your mindset is positive, it is the perfect time to undertake an important activity.

Repeat daily to create significant impact. Success needs discipline and repetition.

This action sheet guides you through the first 4 steps. Set yourself a 7-day challenge to complete this each day for the next week. Then look to maintain and extend the streak.

60 SECOND STATE CHANGER
ACTION SHEET
(REPEAT DAILY)

GiFT631
#WHATWINNERSDO

WRITE DOWN YOUR SMUUT GOAL

WRITE DOWN YOUR CHOSEN AFFIRMATION/ MANIFESTATION

WRITE DOWN 2/3 THINGS YOU ARE HAPPY + GRATEFUL FOR TODAY

1.

2.

3.

WRITE DOWN SOMETHING YOU ARE PROUD OF (BIG OR SMALL)

26) The GiFT of visualisation

When we discussed desired future state thinking and SMUUT goals, we talked about visualisation. This was brought to life with the goal setting exercise when we considered being on stage picking up an award of our choice.

This is big picture visualisation or dream state visualisation. Allow your mind to wander for a few minutes a day. See your family living your desired future life. See images of experiences you are yet to enjoy and things you are yet to achieve in your life. Visualise what it would be like to be the CEO of your life, enjoying the time/ financial freedom that it brings. The more this movie plays in your mind, the more real and achievable it seems and the more exciting it becomes. Avoid looking to control this visualisation—it is free time for your mind to wander.

There are other ways in which visualisation can be a powerful tool to help our daily mindset and focus our energy and attention.

Before any significant activity, visualise two things. First, the desired outcome you want to achieve from the particular activity, and secondly, visualise a previous occasion in which you completed the same activity to the best of your ability. This centres you, focuses your mind, and allows you to feel in control of your emotions. It also lifts your energy and powers your belief system.

The activity can be different, but this set up should the same. It could be setting up for a presentation, team meeting, customer meeting or sales pitch. It could be speaking in front of people for the first or the 100th time. It could be a critical phone or zoom call. It could be a job interview or meeting with your boss, investors, or a teacher.

Once you have done this visualisation set up, think about the practical element of what you are about to do. I am a believer in focusing on both the opening and the close.

The rest of the activity flows from a brilliant opening as you feel more confident and in control.

Find your own space to do this. Breathe to control your excitement (a better way to think about the activity than focusing on your nerves – thank you to presentation, language and media training expert Bill McFarlan for this top tip) and think about what you want to say and do.

Avoid—and certainly don't be one of—those people who rush from activity to activity and look/act flustered and unprepared at the start of meetings and other activities. You only get a few seconds to make the right first impression; acting/looking even a little flustered or out of control impacts your confidence and the others' confidence in you. Start strongly and avoid the need to recover.

For example, just before I go on stage, I do 4 things:

1) I avoid as much human contact as possible so I can breathe and centre myself.

2) I mentally rehearse my opening and my close.

3) I think back to the best conference speech I have ever given, which energizes me.

4) I pick out two people in the audience and visualise their reactions to the end of my speech. I see the two people turning to each other, praising my speech, nodding in agreement, and smiling. I see the words 'that was amazing' and 'wow' coming out of their mouths.

Practical visualisation is one of the habits that takes effort to get out of the cave and stay there as it needs time, practice and discipline. The impact, once mastered, is powerful.

It is also important to visualise and mentally practice your close. This is how you will be remembered when you leave the room, the zoom call finishes, the phone goes down, or you walk off stage.

What do you want to say last?

How do you want to look and feel?

What do you want others to be saying, thinking and doing in the moments after you finish?

The final form of visualisation ensures I end the day thinking positively about the best things that have happened that day—the gold amongst the glitter.

27) The GiFT from the glitter

During one of my virtual #whatwinnersdo programmes, I described my end of day process.

This is a 90 second process—quick, easy, and when consistently practiced, one that has both reflective and progressive qualities. First, I recall the best things that have happened during the day, then I reflect on something I have learned, and finally, I prepare for the next day by thinking about one thing I am going to focus on. This could be an overarching behaviour, such as helping others, practicing gratitude, giving praise, contacting 10 clients, or writing and posting content on all social platforms. It helps me reflect, unwind, and end the day on a positive note, while also setting the tone for the following day.

I am told and have read that the subconscious mind is always working, even when we sleep. That being said, I think it is crucial to manage my thoughts before going to sleep. I ensure that I avoid social/news feeds at this time, as I want to remove any negative stimuli. I know others like to rewrite their goals at this time, while some either rewrite or reread their affirmations. Both are also great winning habits if they do not stimulate your mind at a time when you need to relax and recharge through a deep sleep.

A friend from Copenhagen, Pernille Hartmann, participated in this virtual #whatwinnersdo programme.

After the live session finished, Pernille contacted me and referenced a Danish actress, speaker, author, and filmmaker named Hella Joff. Hella says that you can never get too much glitter in your life and encourages people to take the best experience of the day, add glitter, and place it by the fireplace in your mind.

When I heard this, I immediately started to implement it into my evening routine. Just before I am going to sleep, I close my eyes and visualise a roaring log fire. I see glitter falling in front of the fire, and amongst it is the gold from my day. It is a beautiful image that helps me sleep and ensures the day ends superbly. While sleeping, my inner champion is thinking positive thoughts, so I wake up ready for my 4M routine to begin again.

Questions for you:

How do you normally sleep?

How do you end your day to prepare for a great sleep?

How and when do you reflect on the day?

Actions for you:

Complete this simple exercise every day for 7 days before you move to the next GiFT:

1. What was the best thing that happened today?

2. What have I learnt today?

3. What is your No1 focus for tomorrow?

4. Describe the glitter from your day......either write this out in your journal or close your mind, see the roaring log fire and the glitter falling amongst the gold.

28) The GiFT of symbols and images

As you have seen from previous GiFTs I believe in the importance of symbols. Symbols trigger emotional responses. Like most people I have met, I am a confidence player and I like to leave nothing to chance regarding my mindset and belief system. Therefore, having symbols that create a positive emotional response is helpful. Everywhere I go, I take a Yoda keyring and miniature toy rhino with me. They speak to me without ever talking.

At times, we hit barriers and have disappointments. Our energy is in danger of draining and our commitment is tested. This is where and when Yoda and the rhino come in. They give me confidence and help improve my self-talk, which is critical to ensuring my mindset remains optimistic and positive.

Yoda reminds me that our "focus is reality" and that "there is no try. Do or do not."

The rhino needs a little more explanation.

When I accepted my first senior leadership role, I was placed in charge of a difficult and challenging business that had underperformed for a considerable period. I was young, energetic, determined, and passionate, yet I felt like I was constantly running into brick walls. Some days, I saw no progress and believed I was going nowhere.

One day, my colleague, David Koziupa, came into our shared office and put an article down on the table in front of me. "I think you should read this," he said. So, I did. And the article had a profound impact on my life and career.

The article was about rejecting mediocrity and focused on the characteristics of a rhino as opposed to a cow. The rhino kept moving forward and was strong, determined, and persistent. The cow settled for mediocrity, chewing grass contentedly in the meadows and watching the world pass by. I termed it **#rhinorationale**. Success is about pace, urgency, direction, and momentum. In challenging times, it is also about resilience and persistence, as well as the ability to overcome barriers, setbacks, and disappointments.

As I said earlier, I keep a miniature toy rhino with me everywhere. I also have rhino pictures, carvings, and ornaments all over my office and other places I frequently visit. They act as a constant reminder to be thick skinned, determined, and to keep moving forward even in challenging times. From this, **#sempreavanti** was born.

29) The GiFT of #s

Not all symbols need to be physical objects. The consistent use of #s when I post on social media (normally LinkedIn) and communicate in other ways with my audience is another form of symbols. The good news is I do not need to carry them with me or have them sitting on my desk! Their impact however is just as positive.

Each time I use the following #s, I am talking to myself just as much as I am talking to my audience. The #s remind me of who I am, what I stand for, and where I am going. The more I write them, the more influence they have on my inner champion and belief system. The message goes deeper into my subconscious.

As you read through my most common #s, have your journal in hand. Take a moment to reflect and think as you read. Scribble down any words/phrases of your own that come to mind:

#sempreavanti - Italian for *always forward*.

As stated in the last GiFT, this reminds me to keep moving forward toward my goals, stay focused, and operate within my circle of influence. It reminds me to get up when I am knocked down, dust myself off, and keep going. There is no time to feel sorry for myself and no value in procrastination. This # reminds me to make decisions and act. If a mistake is made, learn and go again.

#time2soar #dare2soar

My company logo is a simple design of an eagle flapping its wings. It fits my purpose of helping people strive to reach their true potential by being the wind beneath their wings, so they soar to new heights. I use the eagle emoji along with these two #s. One reminds me there is no better time than the present to take decisive, goal-focused action, while the other reminds me to stay out of the cave and to have the courage to set bigger SMUUT goals.

#winner2winner #eagle2eagle

Winners attract winners and players attract players. The energy we put out is the energy we receive. The first # reminds me to seek out great people who I can learn from as well as give to. As Jim Rohn articulates, we become the sum of the 5 to 6 people we spend most time with, therefore, it is critical that we choose these people wisely.

During one of my virtual #whatwinnersdo programmes, Sim Riley in England spoke with Almas Taufiq in Pakistan, and they linked the #winner2winner expression to my purpose and business logo reframing it as #eagle2eagle. I immediately jumped onto this and constantly look for other eagles – people who are going to help me soar to even greater heights.

I met Manny Martinez in Olympia, Washington State, USA through LinkedIn. He quickly became my #eagle2eagle partner during the early days of the Covid-19 pandemic when I needed to associate with people who were happy, positive, and optimistic. People who could be the wind beneath my wings during difficult times. Manny and I are yet to physically meet but we have built a strong relationship and growing friendship, where we share ideas, have fun and believe in each other.

In this connected world, the eagles in your life can be anywhere across the globe. Find them!

#allin

When I decide to do something, I commit. I am all in. This # reinforces the need to give 100% to everything I take on so I can set and go after SMUUT goals. It is about living to my potential and being the best I can be. This # also reminds me not to overcommit as you cannot be #allin when you have too much on your plate. It is about doing less, better. It is about doing what matters most.

#whatwinnersdo and #futureyou – for context.

These are the titles of my events, my journal, and my membership community.

#whatwinnersdo is the name shared by my events and my journal. The events cover many of the GiFTs from this book and are designed to provide attendees with the simple, practical and actionable tools they need to move forward in life. It follows the GiFT631 success formula, like this book. The journal carries the same name and consists of many of the mindset practices covered here.: the 4M morning routine, affirmations, 1+3+6 process, along with space to complete your be amazing list and what you are happy/grateful for.

#futureyou is my international membership community. It is designed to help people develop the skills and confidence to move from where they are to where they want to be (i.e., your desired future state or #futureyou). It is a mix of blogs, interviews, trainings, and communications. It is a super group full of those with an #eagle2eagle mentality like those who have added their contributions to this book.

Linked to the #giiftbites on the YouTube channel, Andy Fell, GiFT631, it is a complete personal success system.

Questions for you:

What physical symbols do you carry with you?

Where else do you have them? Your office, desk, in your car?

What emotional responses do they trigger?

Along with the physical symbols, what other techniques do you use?

What expressions or 'mottos' sum you up?

How, when, and where do you use them?

What social media do you use?

How do your posts speak back to you as well as to your audience?

Actions for you:

Let's have some fun and create some #s.

Be creative and avoid over-thinking.

In 2 minutes come up with as many #s as you can that reflect you and how you want to live:

\# ....

\# ....

\# ....

\# ....

\# ....

\# ....

\# ....

\# ....

\# ....

\# ....

Leave this exercise for 24 hours.

Come back to the list the next day.

Add to it, delete the ones you do not think work for you and amend others to have more meaning.

Pick your top 5/6:

\# ....

\# ....

\# ....

\# ....

\# ....

\# ....

Start using them as frequently as you can.

By now you should be building your success system through the repeated use of disciplines like rewriting your goals, your affirmations, be amazing list and the other techniques. Your screensavers, vision board, journaling and daily routines help extend the system.

The repeated use of these #s, along with some physical symbols add another layer to the system.

Once set up and established, all are simple, practical, and quick!

30) #Give2get becomes #GiFT2get

There is one # I have kept out of the previous exercise as it is based on a life philosophy. It came out of one of my greatest learnings and early failings.

There was a time when I lost sight of my grandfather's beliefs and I became too focused on what I wanted to GET from a meeting or conversation. I would go into a meeting with a team member thinking about how I could get the other person to perform better as opposed to thinking about how I could do more to help and support them. This mindset also applied to meetings with customers. I focused on what I could do to GET more of their business, as opposed to what I could do to help them achieve their goals or satisfy their needs. With a business partner, I focused on how I could GET a better deal, as opposed to how we could help each other achieve our respective goals.

I was totally focused on the GET.

During my Mozart time, I began to reflect on my grandfather's teachings and the person I wanted to become. I realised I needed to make a simple but profound change to my approach. I needed to focus on what I could GIVE. This sounds so simple, but it takes discipline—a winning habit that requires energy and effort. It is a form of servant leadership and starts with the simple question:

What more can I do to help?

Once I mastered this, I found that everything else improved, including my team's performance, the quality of customer conversations, and a shift in supplier relationships from transactional to partnership.

Living and leading from a position of helping others impacts all those around you as it is a very positive approach to life and business. It is conducive to building belief, confidence and trust. It encourages others to leave their cave and seek to move forward. People know you are there to help and support them and you want to be the wind beneath their wings. It draws people towards you and ensures you have richer and more rewarding conversations. In turn, this fuels your desire to have a bigger impact on others. As you feel better, your attitude becomes ever more positive, and you feel rewarded and enriched. It is a highly virtuous cycle.

Born out of this thinking came one of my mantras: **#give2get.** You focus on the GIVE without any expectation on the GET. However, over time you find the more you GIVE the more the GET looks after itself.

When I read John O'Leary's 'On Fire' after my 50th birthday it explained brilliantly how this approach to people had been core to John's happiness, fulfilment, and success. I recommend the book and the approach. It is so aligned to my grandfather's teachings and my success as a leader.

I also believe it sets a tone where others want to help you as much as they can. This help comes in so many ways.

At a recent #whatwinnersdo event in Edinburgh, Scotland I was talking about this approach when one of the participants Kevin Smith recommended, I change #give2get to **#GiFT2get** so it fitted with my business name and philosophy. As with so much of my content, by sharing it, people see things you don't. You get new learnings as well as different perspectives. I learned, adapted and added a new 10% to this manta. It is the precious GiFT of feedback.

It is why you #give2get or now #GiFT2get.

31) Lily's GiFT

Leona and I had just returned from a business trip to Las Vegas when she asked me about the day ahead. I was tired, had enjoyed a little too much red wine, and replied: "I have an ugly day tomorrow." Little did I know that my youngest daughter Lily, who was only 7 years old at the time was listening.

It was a rare slip out of the player mindset and proof that there is a little bit of the victim mindset in all of us.

The next morning, I was on the ferry to Sydney's Circular Quay when I noticed a text sent from Leona's phone. It read, "Hi Daddy. I miss you so much. **Be amazing** at work today. Forget about an ugly day. Think of a happy day. Love you lots and lots. See you soon. Lily!"

Given Lily's age, I assumed the message was from Leona pretending to be Lily to make me smile and raise my energy for the day.

And so, I decided to play along. "I will think happy. Thanks for the coaching moment, Lily," I responded.

A reply came immediately, "It's okay. Last night you said today was going to be an ugly day. Life is too short to have ugly days. Can't wait to see you tonight."

At the time, Lily ended every conversation with a muscle emoji because she teased me for not having any. That was when I realised it was from her and not Leona. I was shocked how a seven-year-old had not only picked up on my rare slip into a poor-quality mindset, but had also cared enough to message me, coach me, and fire me up.

Lily was being the wind beneath my wings. The message and sentiment behind it had a huge impact on how I was feeling in the moment. My energy and confidence soared. As with Audrey's marathon email, I always keep the message and the sentiment with me.

'Life is too short for ugly days.'

32) The GiFT of changing the song

The previous GiFT evidences you can easily slip from the player mindset when tired. It also shows the risk that a poor choice of language can create an impact on those around you. I recommend you read *'Drop the Pink Elephant'* by Bill McFarlan to understand how to improve your language to improve the quality and impact of your communication as well as your own mindset.

If you slip out of the player zone you are setting a tone where others can follow you.

Sometimes without realising it, a seemingly trivial thing can also make an impact.

Let's contrast the positive impact from Leona's song, the screen-saver, dashboards, and trophies with a habit I fell into for a short period of time. Each morning, I walked around the house in Sydney singing the opening lines from the Madness song, "Grey Days."

"In the morning I awake, my arms, my legs, my body aches...so begins another weary day."

It was contagious and before long, I could hear other members of the family singing it, too. Maybe it was reminding me of my youth in England when I loved bands like Madness, the Jam, and the Specials. Whatever the reason, it is not how I wanted to start the day and not how I wanted those around me to think, believe, and feel. It was setting the wrong tone.

I love the start of the day when the world comes alive, and I am at my most creative and productive. My state needs to match my energy as I need to attack my goals and get things done. All the great work from the 4M routine and other winning habits/routines can be easily undone in such a way.

It is not just the music I listen to.

It is distancing myself from all forms of negative influence. This includes limiting the amount of news, tv shows and social feeds I consume. It also means choosing who I spend my time with wisely. I was once asked a question at a #whatwinnersdo event about negative influences and people. I answered in this manner:

"It is very hard to live the life of your dreams and achieve big goals when you allow negative influences to upset and disturb your mindset. Why spend time with people who criticise, complain, and always see the downside in situations? These are the people who live in a river of self-doubt and have given up on their dreams. Why spend any time swimming with them?"

Before we move on, identify the things you're doing—or not doing—that are negatively impacting your life. This may even be something as trivial as a song you sing to yourself that can be sending the wrong messages to your subconscious. Think about any negative self-talk or negative visualisation. Replace them with positive triggers and thoughts. Use the state changer and/or the individual elements like affirmations or your **be amazing** list, look at your vision board, your screensaver, meditate, or schedule in a coffee with the most positive and uplifting person from your winning circle.

By the way, I still love Madness but I erased *"Grey Days"* from my internal playlist.

Questions and actions:

What are you doing that negatively impacts on your mindset? Who is negatively influencing your mindset?

Capture these impacts now:

1. ....
2. ....
3. ....
4. ....
5. ....
6. ....

What could you do to replace these negative impacts with more positive actions?

How can you change your relationship with those you need 'to love from a distance' or just spend less/no time with?

In need, think back through the GiFTs in this chapter and/or add your own ideas and thoughts:

1. ....
2. ....
3. ....
4. ....
5. ....
6. ....

33) Mindset summary – the GiFT of the mindset mountain

Achieving our desired future state and bringing our dreams to life requires a clear purpose, a series of SMUUT goals, and consistent high value action. To keep us on that journey, there is a series of techniques we can use to improve our confidence and belief system. Essentially, they fuel our inner champion, overpower our inner critic, and ensure we approach life with a positive attitude and mindset. As my #eagle2eagle friend, Manny Martinez, states, "Setbacks are then merely setups for the comeback."

There is a lot in this section. I believe there needs to be as so much of our ability to achieve success and move in the direction we want to go is dependent on our mindset.

To summarise this section, I want to demonstrate how we can build a champion mindset by using the GiFT631 mindset mountain.

The 4 foundation levels are non-negotiable. The levels in the middle are the portfolio of options as described in this section of the book. Ideally, we create a series of winning habits and routines to practice these disciplines daily. We can use what is provided to us, such as the content of the *#whatwinnersdo* journal, the 4M routine, and the state changer, or we can learn, adapt, and then add 10% to create our own.

The opportunity is to create a compelling series that works for you. The risk is that until this becomes engrained in your behaviour, then it is easy to fall back down the mountain. At times like this, the summit seems much further away.

We will complete this activity together to reinforce what we have covered in this section and encourage you to start thinking about how you create your own winning activities and routines.

Activity:

1. Draw a triangle, shaped like a mountain.

2. Draw 11 straight lines across the interior of the triangle so you have 12 spaces to write in.

3. In the top space, essentially the summit of the mountain, write SMUUT goals. This is your achieving your desired future state and living the life of your dreams. Your SMUUT goals are there to give you a sense of purpose and direction to enable you to focus your climb.

4. Then go to the bottom level. Write in sleep/hydration/nutrition. In the space above write movement. I believe these are 4 essential elements to a healthy mindset. I see you need these elements in place to establish a base camp.

5. We now have our summit and a strong basecamp. We can now add the following climbing techniques in any order you wish. These are the areas we have focused on in this book. In the spaces in between add:

- Meditation
- Journaling/Mozart time
- Gratitude/Appreciation
- Affirmation
- Winning circle (creating your #eagle2eagle group)
- 'Be amazing' list
- Symbols and Images (physical/#s)
- Visualisation
- Visual Representation

6. Take some Mozart time to think about combinations that might work for you. Look back to the 4M morning routine or the state changer. When you add a number of these techniques together you can create a powerful daily routine to power up your inner champion and fuel your mindset and belief system. Feel free to add in anything practical like the mind-cleanse stage in the 4M routine.

7. Write out what the combination you want to practice (e.g., movement – affirmations – gratitude – be amazing list).

8. Commit to a time to make this happen. Add it to your diary.

9. Some messages, like Audrey's email and Lily's text, will be personal to you. Collect them, keep them, use them to supplement the

techniques contained within the mindset mountain. They have a deep meaning and can make a huge difference in the moments when your inner critic is eating away at your confidence.

I have added a blank mindset mountain to set up the process for you.

MINDSET MOUNTAIN

One the next page is a completed mindset mountain. You can shuffle the middle sections as you want. Feel free to add anything that helps you.

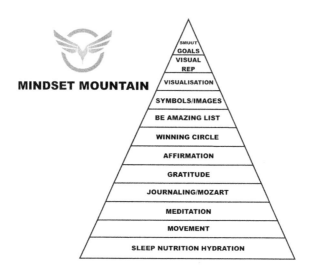

In this final version I have added the frameworks I use to help me make consistent progress in the direction of my SMUUT goals.

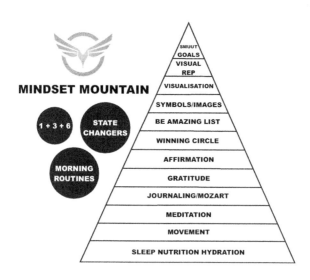

As you have seen there is some significant overlap between the goals and the mindset section. The GiFT631 success formula is inter-linked. One thing that is guaranteed is that you will get you nowhere without ACTION. This is the focus for section 4.

SECTION 4
ACTION

As Arnold Schwarzenegger said, "You cannot climb the ladder of success with your hands in your pockets". You can set SMUUT goals, and work to improve your mindset to ensure your belief system is strong. However, to move forward, you must take consistent, high value action.

Not all action is the same, as evidenced by the time in which I was caught up in the whirlwind of life and business. You can be busy and still go nowhere.

I believe people frequently know what they need or want to do, they know how to do it and they know why they want or have been asked to do it. The challenge for many is the 'when' to do it.

When coaching the Sheffield Sharks Basketball team in the UK, Coach Jim Brandon shared his *no drift* philosophy with me. If he saw that members of the team weren't starting a game with the intensity he wanted, he would call a time-out, gather the team together in a huddle, and reset expectations. I believe we all need a *no drift* policy in our lives. So, be willing to call your own time-out—a short burst of *Mozart time* to stop, think, and reassess.

I only have two settings in life and business: stillness and speed. The stillness is Mozart time and includes these short, sharp, time-outs. This is followed by intense bursts of high value, high focus activity. One goes hand in hand with the other.

The stillness is the thinking time to ask myself questions, to consider and make decisions. Without it there is a great chance that you can be acting with speed but going in the wrong direction. Being slightly off course at a journey's beginning, can become a serious problem over time if unaddressed. Hence the need to not only have some Mozart time up front but to reflect on and debrief the action you have taken.

To focus my mind and ensure I avoid any drift, there are four comments I have put on my office wall, directly in my eye line.

The first is taken from the US swimmer, Michael Phelps, in which he says, "What matters *now*?" This is a focusing question and ensures I refocus on the high value. I added a second question to this: "What matter most?" to ensure my action is high value AND focuses on my purpose and/or SMUUT goals.

The third is from another swimmer, the Australian Grant Hackett, OAM. It was Grant who shared the Michael Phelps question with me. At the same time, he added his own expression to it: "Whatever it Takes." At times, the waters will be choppy and this is when you need this philosophy. You need to work the choppy waters of the messy middle. It directly relates to and reinforces some of my # mantras: having a #rhinorationale approach, being #allin with a #sempreavanti way of thinking.

Finally, I added "prevent procrastination", which is an expression used by Royston Guest. It reminds me to move to action without overthinking. One way I do this is through my D-C-Go approach which starts this section.

34) The GiFT of D-C-Go!

Why does procrastination and overthinking kill dreams, opportunities, and business ideas?

People convince themselves that the time isn't right. They convince themselves that they don't have enough time or money, that conditions aren't right, that they don't have the required skills, the right team, or the right level of security. Others seek perfection before they take any decisive action. When this *spectator* mindset creeps in, it feeds self-doubt and the fear of what *might* happen. Venturing out of the cave to see what lies outside is risky. Rather than taking this risk confidently, some people become too cautious and inactive. Most stay in or head back to the cave. People stick with jobs they do not enjoy, continue to work for a boss who does not treat them well, and stick around at a company that does not value what they do. Hopes and dreams are pushed to the side for a day that never comes.

If you're in a similar situation, how do you overcome this?

First, decide what to you want to achieve. Write it down with absolute clarity. It is the G part of the success formula. Get clear on where you want to go in life and business. Set some clear goals. Make them SMUUT goals.

Then, before you start, ask yourself a simple and critical question: *How committed am I to the achievement of this goal/task/project?*

To answer this question and measure your level of commitment, give yourself a score out of 10—with 10 being the highest form of commitment. If you are giving yourself less than a 9, why start?

Only start things that really matter, move you forward, and make you happier than you are today. Many initiatives fizzle out because of a lack of commitment. When the going gets tough, it's easy to give up on something you are not entirely dedicated to, wasting time, money, and the goodwill of everyone else involved in your project, task or goal.

The expression that we need to "do more, better with less" is too frequently used in business. I used to say it constantly. However, I now believe we must flip this thinking. To be successful and build the life we want, we must "do less, better with more". Do **fewer** things (and only those you are really committed to) with greater meaning, so you go after them with **more** passion, energy, drive, and commitment.

When fully committed, you will find a way and you will hold yourself accountable to a higher standard.

Once I pass this internal commitment test, I take immediate action. I go. I am **#allin.** I take my first action quickly. Avoiding immediate action is risky. When you procrastinate, you overthink and start to second guess yourself. You are in danger of talking yourself out of it completely. Your self-talk becomes 'I'll start tomorrow.' Or 'I need to do this, have this or get this and then I will start.' Tomorrow comes and goes. It then becomes the next day and the next day and eventually you become a 'gonna.'

'I was gonna do it, but life got in the way!"

In essence**, Decide - Commit - GO! (D-C-Go!)**

Friend and client, Kevin Griffen, recommended adding *execute* to this simple model. His feedback was as follows, "Getting going is great, but finishing is even better!" To execute and complete what you have started, apply the 1+3+6 model. This keeps your actions focused and relevant. It keeps you going and moving forward.

35) The GiFT of time blocking!

After my 4M morning routine and act of appreciation my mindset is positive, focused, and strong. It is a great time to be doing 'deep work'. Deep work is high value work requiring some committed time. For example, it could be work on a key project, writing a client proposal, a speech, a blog or a chapter of this book. It could be doing something that has been captured in my mind-cleanse, preparing for a critical client meeting or reviewing some documentation.

This realisation came from the recommendation to listen to *The One Thing* audiobook by Gary Keller. One thing I have learnt—when you access great and highly impactful content—is to read/listen to a resource more than once. Each reread or re-listen deepens your understanding of the core concepts and thinking. It is amazing how frequently new learnings emerge on a second or third read.

I have accessed *The One Thing* numerous times, and each time, it provides me with new lessons and new knowledge.

Critical to my daily success system is that I now schedule time for the most important activity of the day (my "one thing") straight after my morning routine. 'One thing time' is my name for the deep work

I need to do that day. If my schedule is already booked, I make sure I keep one clear space in my dairy each day to do my "one thing." Since I am self-employed, I block extended periods of *"one thing" time*—usually on a Monday—to get the week off to a good start. It is also the time when my clients want to hear from me least, so it is a perfect match.

Whatever happens after this time, I avoid the "where did my day go?" or "what did I actually achieve today?" internal monologue. Recall the Goethe saying, "The things that matter most must never be at the mercy of the things that matter least."

Questions for you:

Do you control your diary or does your diary control you?

Do you feel in control of time or does time seem to control you?

When do you do your 'deep work'? (This could even work for your key passion projects like exercise, painting, learning Spanish, playing the guitar).

What simple changes can you make to start gaining control and doing more of what matters most when you feel at your best?

What activities are getting in the way? What changes can you make to stop or reduce their impact?

Action for you:

1) Look at your diary for the next month.

2) Start to time-block some time for your deep-work.

3) Do it at a time that works for you and when your energy is high.

4) If you need help with what matters most, work through the following GiFT to help your thinking about where and what to focus on.

36) The GiFT of high value action

Do you have a high value or high-performance diary? When you look at your schedule and how you have set yourself up, do you believe it is full of the activities needed to ensure you focus on your SMUUT goals and achieve a happy, successful, and fulfilling life?

The introduction of time-blocking in the last GiFT was an attempt to create space in your schedule to do what matters most. Too many people are so busy being busy and see time as being outside of their control. They work hard without moving forward as they want. This can mean they slip out of the player mindset and into a cynical/ victim mindset when everything appears 'too hard' to change.

The following is a simple activity, but one that bears tremendous fruit when relentlessly applied. It creates efficiency, capacity, and enhanced performance in all aspects of life and work. It can help you focus on the 'one thing' time to ensure it bears fruit.

To start, simply draw a line down the middle of a page in your journal or workbook.

To the left of the line, write the heading: High Value Activities (HVAs)

To the right of the line, write the heading: Low Value Activities (LVAs)

Start with the left-hand column. Under this heading, list the 3-5 highest value activities you need to do to deliver success in your work or personal life.

Think about a week (or a longer period if you need to). Ask yourself this question: "What percentage of your working time do you spend on these activities?"

Then, move to the right-hand column. Under this heading, list the 3-5 lowest value activities you're doing. These have a low impact, low meaning, and clearly do not move you in the direction of your goals.

Again, answer the question: "What percentage of your working time do you spend on these activities?"

Let's consider the example of a sales professional. Their 4 highest HVAs are:

1. Making appointments

2. Pre-calls to set up the appointment for success

3. Conducting appointments

4. Following up on appointments to deliver on promises and commitments

Their 4 lowest LVAs are:

1. Sales administration

2. Endless sales meetings (often with no set agenda, clear actions, or minutes taken)

3. Sales reporting (more time reporting activities than actually doing the activities)

4. Travel time

Once you identify the LVAs, it becomes easier to consistently reduce or eliminate the amount of time spent on them. We can seek alternative and more efficient ways of doing them—if we even need to do them at all. We can then increase the amount of time spent on the high value activities. These tend to be activities that we enjoy, thus making us more engaged with what we are doing, and we do it better over time as we are more focused on these areas with less distractions.

Look again at your low value activities.

Take each one in turn.

Do you need to do it at all?

Can you find a way to do it more efficiently?

Can you find someone else more suited to the activity to do it for you?

Can you delegate or outsource the activity?

If you believe you do need to do it, when are you doing it?

Can you reschedule it for a time more suitable for low value activities?

I have provided an action sheet to help you work through this GiFT of time:

HIGH VALUE ACTION
ACTION SHEET

GiFT631
#WHATWINNERSDO

HVA	LVA
%	%
ACTIONS TO INCREASE	ACTIONS TO DECREASE

37) The GiFT from the 'debate'

When should you make key decisions and start to take decisive high value action? When energy is high, and you feel in a positive mindset.

What should you do when tiredness sets in and our energy is depleted? Rest, switch off, go for a walk, read a book or if you need to get things done ensure they are from the low value list. This is the time to do some of the things on your mind-cleanse that you did not star.

One of my early childhood memories centres on my dad and grandad sitting around a table at 631, having deep and seemingly heated discussions. When I asked my dad why they argued so much, he countered by saying they were debating. One debate ended with my grandad telling my dad, "Things always look better in the morning."

Throughout my life, I have often reflected on my grandad's wise words.

I have learned to avoid making decisions and taking high value action when I am tired. I would extend this thinking further to consider this approach when planning an important phone call, sending an email or engaging in any other form of written communication. Rather than the mentality of, "I just need to get this off my desk, out of my inbox, or checked off before I go home", wait and reassess. If it is an email, use your draft box and put a reminder on your mind-cleanse list to look at it in the morning.

I see things with much greater clarity and think more clearly when I feel fresh, and I believe you will be the same.

As Jack Welsh, the legendary leader of GE once said: "Manage energy, not time."

Questions for you:

Now you have a better sense of what is high value and what is low value, challenge yourself:

Do you have a system to ensure you do HVAs when you are fresh and full of energy?

Are you in essence, matching energy to value?

Equally are you completing the LVAs such as what you did not star or tick on your mind-cleanse when you have completed your HVAs and when your energy is lower?

What changes can you make to how you are operating?

38) Malcolm's forever GiFT

The best advice I have ever been given came from a legendary leader in my life, my long-term boss, Malcolm McDowell.

Early in our time working together, Malcolm shared the following advice:

"Do the job you are doing today as if you will be doing it forever."

His words were so simple and yet so powerful. Adopting this mentality allowed me to make all the right decisions for both the short- and long-term. It helped me avoid cutting corners in hopes of getting quick results. It allowed me to uncover the root cause of the issues I was experiencing. Instead of applying band-aid solutions, this piece of advice aided me in finding and implementing the best solutions I could. It reinforced the need to focus on high value actions as they are the ones that make a difference. It focused me on hiring the best people I could afford in every role and to work hard to develop a high performing team. I thought about my own development along with that of the team focusing on my behavioural as well as technical skills.

This advice reinforced the need to decide – commit – Go as procrastination and hesitation does not help the person doing a job forever! Equally overcommitting and seeing initiatives fizzle out or being done poorly is counterproductive to long-term, sustainable success and happiness.

Crucially this piece of advice allows you to be guided by purpose, vision, and legacy.

Questions and actions for you:

Whenever you need to test your actions, test them against this advice.

If you were doing what you are currently doing forever, would you take the proposed course of action?

Think back to some earlier questions we used in a different context to help you. If you were to do what you are currently doing forever:

What would you start doing?

What would you stop doing?

What would you do differently? What would you do to a higher standard?

What would you do more of?

Who's help would you enlist? Why? For what purpose?

39) The business card GiFT!

One day, Malcolm had my business card on his desk. My official title at the time was sales co-ordinator. He picked up the card, looked at it, and then ripped it up, throwing the pieces over his shoulder.

He turned to me and said, "I don't pay people to co-ordinate things. I pay people to manage things."

From that day forward, I managed things. There was no time to be a *spectator* in Malcolm's world—he expected decisiveness and action.

In the late 1990s, I wanted my company to sponsor the Sheffield Steelers ice-hockey team. At the time, the company didn't engage in professional sport shirt deals. I passed the case to Malcolm, who told me not to hold out much hope, but he would put it 'up the line' regardless. To my surprise, he came back to me a couple weeks later to say it was approved. I was ecstatic. A great partnership was formed with the Steelers. On a recent visit to Sheffield, over 20 years later, I saw Mike O'Connor, with whom I had done the deal, and we both beamed with happiness when we talked about some of the things we achieved together through that partnership.

About the same time, Malcolm told me he hadn't referred the deal to anyone. He had weighed up the opportunity and the potential risks. He felt it was the right thing to do. He didn't co-ordinate things; he managed things. He made the decision and he gave me the green light.

It was decide – commit – GO with some brilliant execution.

Malcolm sent me a card at the start of the next financial year, which summed up this philosophy. It was hand-written, of course, and quoted Helen Keller: "Life is a daring adventure or nothing at all."

To achieve the life of our dreams and live true to our potential, we need to take risks. To achieve great results and make a big difference we need to back ourselves. We need to have a go and be #allin. We need to stretch far from our cave. To climb a proverbial mountain, where the view from the top is amazing, we need a strong and powerful mindset. We are exposed to the criticism and ridicule of others, so we need to believe in who we are and what we are doing.

It is the risk of winning.

As Elbert Hubbard once said: *'The greatest mistake a person can make is to be afraid of making one!'*

40) The bamboo GiFT

What about when you have stretched from your cave, taken some risks and believe you are taking the right actions..........and nothing seems to happen and no obvious progress is made?

Frank Dick, the one-time British Athletics Coach, said, "Once planted, you can dance around it, sing to it, feed it, water and pray to it—you can do anything you want, and nothing appears to happen. However, once bamboo starts to grow, you just cannot stop it."

Frank was the first person to inspire me to become a conference speaker, leader, and coach. I find him highly motivating, engaging, and practical. He keeps things simple and speaks with absolute clarity. He engages the heart and the mind. I set up *GiFT631* and wrote this book with him in view. I have learned, copied, adapted, and added my own 10% winning edge to many of his teachings.

The bamboo analogy works in several different arenas, from personal growth and business performance, to seeing the results of a new idea. Success takes time and patience. People often expect instant results and give up too soon. All the feeding, watering, and other activities are adding unseen value and are preparing the bamboo to suddenly break the surface and grow at great speed. The risk is we stop these activities too soon because we believe that nothing is happening. We need to keep believing without immediate and visible evidence.

When the bamboo hits the tipping point, there is exponential growth—the investment pays off. I hear this frequently from some of the world's biggest social media names. They set up systems to develop their brand and business, and frequently go unrecognised for a period of time. Overnight sensations are rare. In almost all situations, the work must come first.

The power in many of the GiFTs we have covered is in their consistent use. At times, it feels like the bamboo analogy and results will not happen immediately. Through repetition and the creation of your own winning habits you will hit your own tipping point and see the results of your efforts as you climb the mountain towards the achievement of your SMUUT goals.

Sometimes others can see things you cannot and be able to help you on the way. Friend and mentor, Chris Thomas, shared his belief that "feedback is the breakfast of champions."

Feedback is another critical source of improvement. Make a distinction between feedback that is constructive and well-intentioned, even when it is hard to take and criticism/cynicism. Welcome and accept feedback and avoid criticism/negative comments that add no value. One builds value, one destroys value. One generates confidence, one destroys confidence. One leads to growth and improvement, the other does not.

Why listen to someone with a *cynical* or *victim* mindset? They stopped watering, feeding, dancing, and singing to their own bamboo long ago, and they want you to do the same.

The ability to overcome any sense of pride or ego, which is the enemy of achievement, and listen to quality feedback differentiates you from those who get stuck and are ill-prepared for change.

Actions for you:

When you are yet to see the results of all your efforts, revisit:

- Your vision board and sense of 'why.' Rewrite your desired future state – articulate #futureyou
- Your screensaver and visual images.
- Listen to your chosen song and/or playlist – change it in need.
- Talk to your mentor/coach/winning circle – seek feedback. Have a growth mindset. Be challenged!
- The mindset mountain – do you need to create a new state changer?
- Your morning routine – have you set it up and are you living it daily? Does it help you get into your ideal performance state?
- Your high v low value activity – are you consistently doing what matters most?
- Redo the stage visualisation and the practical stop/start/continue exercise.
- Reread the speech you wrote about how and why you won the award. Rewrite it in need.
- Then, go back to your 1+3+6 framework, rewrite your actions and take the next one. Then the next one and then the next one. #sempreavanti

SECTION 5
DEBRIEFING

___

Gaining clarity on what is high value in terms of activity really matters. The mind-cleanse and HVA v LVA activities are both geared to help give this priority to what matters most. Effective use of our diary by time-blocking everything from Mozart time to deep-work to other key activities like the 15 minutes of thank-you ensure it gets done. Making sure it is prioritised when your energy is high and your mindset is strong, ensures it is done to a high standard.

Feedback from others can be essential part of this journey and accelerate your progress.

Sometimes others are not available or able to provide feedback on these actions. The ability to quickly self-reflect, debrief, extract the learnings, and apply them to the next time you undertake that specific activity or even more broadly is critical.

Richard West who had a long, successful career on the commercial side of Formula One motor racing and then authored *Performance at the Limit* shares the simple 3 step: Plan - Do – Review.

Richard's concern is that he does not see enough planning in life and business, and even less reviewing. Rather life and business are overwhelmed with the 'doing.' Actions can be well intentioned but are not always prioritised and thought through. Then due to a lack of reflection or review the insights and learnings are not captured and integrated into what happens next. Hence people stay caught in a whirlwind of activity without moving in the direction they want to go.

Mozart time helps with the planning but what about the debriefing or reviewing?

Any review or debrief process is about analysing the root cause of success, while also learning from the things that haven't gone as well as we wanted or to plan.

Applying this mentality to the everyday activities we undertake can be done simply and practically. As with all the other GiFTs, it takes consistency to practice and implement even simple debriefing processes. With work, we find the small breakthroughs and take steps forward. Over time the compound effect is significant.

This section provides a series of debrief processes:

1. The first is an in the moment debrief, completed after any significant activity. This helps provide consistent, incremental improvement and can be used to analyse what has gone well (the root cause of success) as well as things that have not.

2. The second is an end of week process, which can be done in 15 minutes. It is ideal for individuals and a great process to create some self-evaluation and improvement across members of a team. I have added the GiFT of a weekly checklist which can supplement this activity or be used in isolation.

3. The third is a bigger process that again works for individuals but also for teams and business units. It can be used at any time, particularly when you are faced with challenges, blockages and feel stuck. It can be repeated as often as needed.

41) The GiFT of active debriefing!

Whenever there is a significant activity to complete, I use my own version of the Plan – Do - Review process. As discussed earlier, I use visualisation to ensure I am in the zone to make a strong and confident start to what is about to happen. This could be a coaching call, sales call, zoom meeting, or conference speech. I call this the set-up.

Once the activity is complete, I spend a few minutes debriefing in the moment, when the emotions are strong, and the feelings are raw. Delaying a debrief can result in blunted memory, lost learnings, and confusion between other activities completed during the day.

Imagine that you are a team leader undertaking 10 coaching meetings a week. You find a 1% improvement on just half of those meetings during the week. Over time, the incremental impact of this continuous improvement is massive (as long as you implement the learnings).

From my time in sales/sales leadership, I observed my team rushing from appointment to appointment. Activity was high, but in terms of results, there was room for improvement. By slowing down the pace a little to implement active set ups and active debriefs, performance improved over time. We slowed down to speed up.

I asked my team, "When does an appointment start?" My team answered that the appointment began 5 minutes prior to its scheduled time. These 5 minutes were set aside to review customer notes and set up an interview room. However, I was hoping that they would answer that these 5 minutes were set aside to allow the individual to get into the ideal performance state though relaxation and active visualization.

Then, I asked, "When does the appointment finish?" to which I initially got an answer that was related to finishing paperwork, administration tasks, or scheduling follow-ups.

The answer I was looking for, however, was, "When I have done my debrief."

The active debrief is a quick process to simply review the following:

What worked well?

What didn't work well?

What could have been done better?

What should I start doing?

What should I stop doing?

What should I do more of and/or do differently?

In this case, supplementary questions may follow, such as:

Which questions were most effective?

How could I create better rapport?

How did I wrap up the conversation and set-up next steps?

Questions for you:

1. What do you do to set up key activities for success?
2. What do you do immediately after a key activity?
3. How do you debrief?
4. If you do a current debrief, when do you do it?
5. Do you analyse the root cause of success as well as disappointment?
6. What do you do with your learnings and insights?

Actions for you:

1. Look at your schedule for the next week/fortnight/month.
2. Ensure you create some space between key activities.
3. Create yourself a template of simple questions you can ask after each key activity.
4. Keep this with you and ensure you work through it each time.
5. Capture at least one key learning per debrief. Use your journal to keep these learnings together.
6. Work through how to integrate it into what you do going forward (use your end of day reflection and your Mozart time as needed).

Let's start now with a basic checklist. You can improve this as you go. It is better to be 66% right and get into activity than waiting until you have something that is 100% perfect.

Pick 4-6 key questions, relating to your key activities that you can use every time:

1. ....
2. ....
3. ....
4. ....
5. ....
6. ....

42) The GiFT of the Friday 15

The *active debrief* is something done in the moment. The *glitter and the gold* is an ideal way to debrief the day and extract the best parts so your subconscious mind thinks about your successes and little wins as you sleep. What about taking a bigger picture view and reviewing the week that just passed?

This process is known as the GiFT631 Friday 15 (F15). It is quick, simple, and powerful, and part of a weekly operating rhythm. All it requires is for you to schedule 15/20 minutes in your diary and have your #whatwinnersdo journal or notebook handy.

Let's set up and work through the activity now.

Look at your diary and block out 15/20 minutes to complete this exercise. Friday is the best day of the week for me to undertake this activity. If your rhythm is different, pick a different day. The key thing is to repeat this once a week. As with other GiFTs, repetition is where the value is found.

Turn off your phone and avoid being in a space where you can be interrupted.

There are 3 key components of the F15 model, all of which are based around a simple series of questions designed to encourage you to do more of what you love (and of what works), reduce what you don't enjoy, and ensure you are focused and organised around your "one thing."

The three areas are as follows:

1. Best,
2. Most challenging, and
3. Next

Answer each question in turn:

Best:

What was the best thing that happened this week?

Why was it the best thing?

What lessons did I learn?

How do I do more of it next week?

Most Challenging:

What has been my most challenging experience this week?

Why was it so challenging?

What did I learn?

How do I reduce the likelihood of it happening again?

Next:

What is *the* most important thing I need to do next week?

Why is it so important?

Two additional questions for you to think about until you create a winning habit:

When is the most important thing scheduled in my diary?

Who's help (if any) do I need to complete it?

From experience, I have found the most important things are frequently not scheduled in people's diaries at all. They are left to chance whereas less important things ARE in the diary. The "one thing" time-block is the ideal time to complete this activity.

I have added an action sheet to enable you to complete this exercise and to provide a template for you to repeat it weekly:

THE FRIDAY 15
ACTION SHEET

GiFT631
#WHATWINNERSDO

BEST

WHAT IS THE BEST THING THAT HAS HAPPENED THIS WEEK?

WHY?

WHAT HAVE YOU LEARNT?

HOW DO YOU DO MORE OF IT NEXT WEEK?

MOST CHALLENGING

WHAT IS THE MOST CHALLENGING THING THAT HAS HAPPENED THIS WEEK?

WHY?

WHAT HAVE YOU LEARNT?

HOW DO YOU REDUCE THE LIKELIHOOD OF IT HAPPENING AGAIN?

NEXT

WHAT IS YOUR NUMBER 1 FOCUS FOR NEXT WEEK?

WHEN? (HAVE YOU ALLOCATED TIME TO DO IT?)

43) The GiFT of a checklist

Soon after starting my daily meeting with Mozart, I found myself writing down questions about how I was leading the team and running my branch. One day, I reread these questions and decided to write them all on the same page. I scribbled "Winners Checklist" across the top and pinned it to the board in front of my desk. I went through these same questions every Friday. It reassured me that I was doing the right things. In essence, I was watering, singing to, and feeding the bamboo—even though I didn't always see the fruit of my labour.

As with every other GiFT in this book, feel free to copy and add your own 10% winning edge to this checklist. Alternatively, feel free to adapt or change it to suit your own needs and those of your team and business. Delete questions that add no value to you, add in questions that do.

The key is to create a guide to help you reflect and debrief during good and bad times.

The Winners Checklist:

- Have you operated 100% within your circle of influence?
- Have you been obsessive about your goals and objectives?
- Have you spent time with those who need you most?
- Have you made your (rising) stars feel great? Have you made recognition a part of your daily routine?
- Have you held your nerve (and done the right things)?
- Have you held your appointment with Mozart?
- Have you learned something new?
- Have you learned from a champion?
- Have you put enough energy into your business?
- Have you done what matters most?
- On a scale of 1-10, how happy are you? (What do you need to do to become a 10?)
- What have you celebrated this week? If so, how? If not, why?

- How much has your business improved between this Friday and the last?

The last question was subjective – it might not be seen in my results but what had I done that I believed would make a difference at a future date. Had I invested in my people, set up lots of client meetings/events, invested in myself, hired a future star, handled a difficult internal situation etc.

44) Removing interference

Are you still struggling to move toward your goals?

Are you still facing internal barriers?

Is your negative self-talk fuelling your inner critic?

Are you still running into concrete obstacles?

What about if the ongoing debrief and F15 are creating incremental improvement but there remain some major blockers getting in your way?

Early in my career, the first external coach I ever worked with GiFTed me a copy of *The Inner Game of Tennis* by Tim Gallwey. One of Tim's core frameworks is performance = potential - interference.

Over time, I adapted this to become Potential - Interference = Performance

Whenever I am stuck or in need of accelerating my performance and progress, I walk myself through this exercise. I also use it with others on a 1:1 basis, with teams and with business units.

The gap between potential and performance is interference. These are the things that are getting in the way, stopping us, and interfering with our performance. They can be in our head (confidence, belief, fear of being judged, etc.) or they can be tangible (paying the bills, time, lack of training, too much low value work, etc.).

First, in your journal, list as many things as you can that you believe are stopping you from improving your performance and reaching your potential. Call this 'your interference.'

Once you have completed an initial list, leave it. During your next scheduled block of time revisit it: add to it, challenge it and refine it as you want and need. Capture as much as you can. Even the process of getting it from your head to your journal is liberating. It often takes a little time to identify and reflect upon the things that are stopping us and interfering with our performance so repeat this stage until you feel you have exhausted the process.

Then, think about 2 circles—the circle of influence and the circle of concern. Those with a *player* mindset spend their whole life within their circle of influence, whereas those with a *victim* and *cynical* mindset spend most of their time talking about things that are of concern but over which they have none or very little influence.

100% FOCUS on WHAT'S WITHIN your CIRCLE of INFLUENCE

To move forward toward our SMUUT goals and our potential, we need to focus on what we can influence.

So, scan the list of interferences. Mark an *I* next to those you can influence, and a *C* next to those that are outside your control.

Strike through those you have put a *C* next to. If you have no control or influence over it, why spend time worrying about it.

Scan the remaining list. Identify 2 entries that you want to tackle first—one should be a quick win and the other should be the most important or significant item of interference. It is important to prioritise the barriers we want to remove first and tackle them one by one. If we focus on too many at a time, we risk not solving anything at all.

Why should one of the first items you pick be a quick win? Well, the brain likes to feel as though we are making progress. It builds confidence and belief. This acts as further fuel for our inner champion. And so, once you have knocked over the quick win, find another. You will find you build momentum as well as confidence. Success does breed success.

Why should one of the first items you pick be the most significant interference? This is because you need to work on it as the solution is a key gateway to success. It is likely to be a much bigger, more time-consuming, and lengthier project.

Then, for the two interferences you have identified, commit to finding a minimum of 2 solutions for each one. Ideally more. The first solution is rarely the best solution as it can be a 'top of the head' thought. Some people need time to think, and a solution may come during their morning movement, journaling, Mozart time, in the shower or even doing a debrief for a seemingly unrelated activity.

Once you have your list of potential solutions, decide which one you are going to utilize.

Decide – commit (give yourself the commitment test) - GO!

Use the 1+3+6 process to break it down so you can focus on the required actions rather than the size of the interference. Take the first action as soon as you can. As a minimum, schedule it to ensure it gets done.

ONE PROBLEM, TWO SOLUTIONS

This exercise can be repeated as many times as needed. As you move toward your SMUUT goals and #futureyou state, you will face new and bigger problems. It evidences you are further from your cave and is a sign of growth and success. New interference, challenges and problems should be welcomed as we now have a full success formula to deal with them!

SUMMARY

The purpose of this book is to help you move from where you are to where you want to be. You now have a series of complementary tools/frameworks/ideas and strategies from which you can build your own success system. By doing this you will gain the confidence to live true to your potential.

Start with the GiFTs that resonate most with you. Build them into how you live your life. Over time, revisit the other GiFTs and ever develop and refine your success system.

Be consistent in your activities to build momentum and evidence the value of the GiFTs. As stated throughout the book, some will work for you as written, some will need you to adapt and add your own 10% to make them yours. I encourage you to do this. What works for me, may not work for you in the exact same format. My only request is you avoid the cynical/spectator and/or victim mindset. Avoid the temptation to explain away why these GiFTs won't work for you. Avoid procrastination and be willing to get out of the cave and act. Give each GiFT long enough to truly uncover the benefits and explore its potential. There are many activities I could have stopped too soon, such as journaling and meditation that now add huge value to my life. Success leaves clues AND mastery takes time as well as effort.

Let's recap.

The book works through the GiFT631 success formula.

Goals give you a real sense of direction and purpose. When you create an emotional connection, they inspire you on the good and the challenging days.

Quite simply our mindset either works for us or against us. We all talk to ourselves, and the question is whether this self-talk fuels our inner champion or our inner critic. The techniques covered are all designed to help build confidence and self-belief, so we stretch ever further from our cave in the direction of our potential and the life of our dreams.

None of this happens without action. As we have seen, not all action is the same. We need to work out what is high value and focus our action when our energy is high and our mindset is strong. Effective use of our diary and when we do what, can make or break the implementation of our success system.

Finally, we need to debrief to drive continuous improvement and accelerate our performance in the direction of our goals and desired future state. #futureyou is out there and accessible for those who have a growth mindset, are willing to accept and implement feedback and then work to get ever better. Often only our ego and our mindset stand in our way!

Whatever your age and current circumstances this book will help you move forward as long as you ACT.

I started with my 50th birthday and a GiFT that began a process that radically changed my life for the better. I end with a story from just over 3 years later. It was the final conversation I had with my dad.

It was a call to action and serves to say that no journey is ever complete. There is more to learn, more to do and more to give. It is my final GiFT to you from my dad's final GiFT to me.

The final conversation: Balsall Common, Coventry, England - December 2019

In late 2019, my father passed away. I had travelled to Balsall Common from Australia's Gold Coast, where I now live, to see him before he passed away. I stayed with my parents at 631, the house I grew up in and after which my business, GiFT631, is named. We both knew this would be our final time together and we had numerous important conversations.

One conversation we had had many times before, but this time, my dad spoke with greater meaning and purpose. He was passing on a message which hit me hard. It took some time to reflect and a walk along a Gold Coast beach with a friend, Nick Bloor, to really understand his intentions and give this conversation greater context.

Dad had been a great cricketer—a quick bowler who also batted with a classical style, taking many wickets and scoring plenty of runs. He was a very handy table tennis player and golfer, too. His cricketing ability led him to being offered a professional contract by Warwickshire in the 1950s. He turned it down, believing he was not talented enough to go beyond county cricket and there wasn't enough money in that level to make a good living.

In his late 50s and early 60s, he was still playing for Berkswell CC—the same club as my brother Philip and me.

I was a promising opening batsman but not as dedicated to the game as my father was. I had trialled for Warwickshire at 15 but did not do myself justice. To be honest, I did not want it enough. I lacked the commitment and determination to reach that level. I enjoyed playing for Berkswell CC in the local league. However, my dad wanted it for me more than I wanted it for myself. He kept pushing me to train harder and be more focused on the game. It was as if he wanted to replay his life through me. It made me realise you cannot want something more than someone wants it for themselves. The more you push, the more they push back.

During one game in the summer of 1983, I was batting, and my dad was umpiring. I had scored 87 runs. Batting was easy, until I hit a poor delivery straight into the hands of a boundary fielder. It was a lazy and terrible shot. I was disappointed in myself as I was 13 runs short of what would have been my first century (100 runs in one innings). As a side note, I scored one shortly afterwards.

My dad told me after the game, the bowler turned to him as the umpire and said, "That lad just threw away a century."

Dad never forgot the bowler's words, the shot I played, or what I threw away in that moment. I believe the incident summed up his feelings about how I wasted the talent I had been given.

Between 1983 and late 2019, Dad raised that shot and told that story so many times. All of my children can retell the story.

It also became our final conversation.

He spoke with more intensity and disappointment than ever before. It became the worst shot he had ever seen from the worst delivery that had ever been bowled. He challenged me hard, asking how I couldn't have seen the fielder and why I put the ball 'straight down his throat'.

The intensity of his words rocked me a little. It was not what I was expecting.

What was he trying to say?

After walking along the beach and talking with Nick, I realised it was not about cricket. Dad was imploring me to use what I had to the best of my ability. It was about finishing what I started. It was my POTENTIAL.

I have not lived up to my potential in sport, business, or life, and he knew this. He was encouraging me in a language we both understood to do better and go for it. I rethink that conversation frequently and replay his words as follows:

"Find the extra 13 runs to finish the job (score a century). Be the best version of you. Be amazing. Use your talents to the maximum and strive to reach your true potential. Live life to the full. Share your GiFTs so others can benefit too.'

Whether this was his intention or not I will never know. What I do know is I live my passion daily. I work hard to become ever better, and I am committed to sharing all I have learnt with others. I am determined to pass my own rocking chair test and I believe the GiFTs in this book will help you do the same.

This book is dedicated to him and all those who have helped me on my journey to date, some of whom are named in this book. Many others have made a difference, some even without knowing. I thank you all.

Printed in Great Britain
by Amazon